Minimum Standards for Education in Emergencies, Chronic Crises and Early Reconstruction

The Inter-Agency Network for Education in Emergencies (INEE) is a global network of over 1,400 individual and organizational members (as of June 2006) who are working together within a humanitarian and development framework to ensure the right to education in emergencies and post-crisis reconstruction. INEE works to improve communication and coordination by cultivating and facilitating collaboration and constructive relationships among its members and strategic partners. The INEE Steering Group provides overall leadership and direction for the network; current Steering Group members include CARE, Christian Children's Fund, the International Rescue Committee, the International Save the Children Alliance, the Norwegian Refugee Council, UNESCO, UNHCR, UNICEF and the World Bank.

INEE's Working Group on Minimum Standards is facilitating the global implementation of the INEE Minimum Standards for Education in Emergencies, Chronic Crises and Early Reconstruction. The INEE Working Group (2005-2008) consists of 20 organizations with education expertise in situations of crisis and early reconstruction: the Academy for Educational Development, BEFARe, CARE India, CARE USA, AVSI, Catholic Relief Services, Foundation for the Refugee Education Trust, Fundación Dos Mundos, GTZ, the International Rescue Committee, Ministry of Education, France, Norwegian Church Aid, Norwegian Refugee Council (NRC), Save the Children USA, UNESCO, UNHCR, UNICEF, USAID, Windle Trust and World Education.

INEE is grateful to more than 22 agencies, institutions and organizations for supporting the network since its inception. For a complete list of acknowledgments, please visit the INEE website: www.ineesite.org.

INEE is open to all interested individuals and organisations who implement, support and advocate for education in emergencies and reconstruction contexts. Interested individuals can sign up for membership through the INEE website: www.ineesite.org. Membership involves no fee or obligation.

For more information, contact INEE:
INEE Network Coordinator, coordinator@ineesite.org
INEE Focal Point on Minimum Standards, minimumstandards@ineesite.org

INEE © 2004
Reprint: INEE © 2006

ISBN 1-58030-034-0

Cover photographs: The International Rescue Committee

Designed and printed by: DS Print|Redesign, London

Contents

For further documentation on assessment forms and checklists, and for links to the Sphere Humanitarian Charter and documents referencing MSEE linkages to Sphere Standards and UNHCR Education Field Guidelines, please go to http://www.ineesite.org/standards/msee.asp and/or see the MSEE CD-ROM, which is available through the INEE website.

Introduction: Minimum Standards for Education in Emergencies, Chronic Crises and Early Reconstruction

The Minimum Standards for Education in Emergencies, Chronic Crises and Early Reconstruction are both a handbook and an expression of commitment, developed through a broad process of collaboration, that all individuals – children, youth and adults – have a right to education during emergencies. They echo the core beliefs of the Sphere Project: that all possible steps should be taken to alleviate human suffering arising out of calamity and conflict, and that people affected by disaster have a right to life with dignity.

Overview

All individuals have a right to education. This right is articulated in many international conventions and documents, including the Universal Declaration of Human Rights (1948); the Convention Relating to the Status of Refugees (1951); the Geneva Convention (IV) Relative to the Protection of Civilian Persons in Time of War; the Covenant on Economic, Social and Cultural Rights (1966); the Convention on the Rights of the Child (1989); and the Dakar World Education Forum Framework for Action (2000), promoting Education For All.

Education is not only a right, but in situations of emergencies, chronic crises and early reconstruction, it provides physical, psychosocial and cognitive protection which can be both life-saving and life-sustaining. Education sustains life by offering safe spaces for learning, as well as the ability to identify and provide support for affected individuals – particularly children and adolescents. Education mitigates the psychosocial impact of conflict and disasters by giving a sense of normalcy, stability, structure and hope for the future during a time of crisis, and provides essential building blocks for future economic stability. Education can also save lives by protecting against exploitation and harm, including abduction, recruitment of children into armed groups and sexual and gender-based violence. Lastly, education provides the knowledge and skills to survive in a crisis through the dissemination of lifesaving information about landmine safety, HIV/AIDS prevention, conflict resolution and peace-building.

Education in Emergencies

In recent years there has been a rise in awareness of the need for non-formal and formal education programmes in emergency situations. Millions of children, youth and adults have benefited from the efforts of education authorities and local and international humanitarian agencies. As more emphasis has been put on education, two important issues have emerged:
1. a recognition that individuals do not forfeit their right to education during emergencies and that education cannot remain 'outside' the mainstream humanitarian debate, but must be seen as a priority humanitarian response; and
2. a broad-based desire and commitment to ensure a minimum level of quality, access and accountability for education in situations of crisis.

In response, in 2003 a working group was constituted to facilitate the development of global minimum standards for education in emergencies. The initiative was hosted within the Inter-Agency Network for Education in Emergencies (INEE), an open network of UN agencies, NGOs, donors, practitioners, researchers and individuals from affected populations working together to ensure the right to education in emergencies and post-crisis reconstruction. The network is responsible for gathering and disseminating good practices, tools and research, promoting the right to education for people affected by emergencies through advocacy, and ensuring the regular exchange of information among its members and partners. INEE also identifies gaps in resources and encourages the development of these resources through Task Teams convened by INEE member organisations.

These global minimum standards are presented in this handbook, which is the result of a broad and consultative process to develop minimum standards for education in emergencies. From 2003 onwards, working with a broad base of stakeholders, the INEE Working Group on Minimum Standards facilitated the development of standards, indicators and guidance notes that articulate the minimum level of educational access and provision to be attained in emergencies, through to the early reconstruction stage. The main components of this development process were national, sub-regional and regional consultations; on-line consultation inputs via the INEE list-serve; and a peer review process. Information gathered from each step was used to inform the next phase of the process.

Over 2,250 individuals from more than 50 countries have contributed to the development of the minimum standards. Between January and May 2004, the INEE Working Group on Minimum Standards facilitated four regional consultations covering Africa, Asia, Latin America, and the Middle East and Europe. The 137 delegates to these regional consultations included representatives from affected populations, international and local NGOs, governments and UN agencies in 51 countries. Prior to the regional consultations, delegates and INEE members coordinated over 110 local, national and sub-regional consultations in 47 countries, gathering input and information from

NGO, government and UN representatives; donors; academics; and over 1,900 representatives from affected communities, including students, teachers and other education personnel. Delegates at the regional consultations built upon the standards, indicators and guidance notes developed at the national and local consultations, as well as over 100 INEE list-serve responses, to develop regional minimum standards. The peer review process that took place during the summer of 2004 involved more than 40 experts who analysed and honed the regional standards into one set of global standards.

The resulting minimum standards are built on the foundations of the Convention on the Rights of the Child (CRC), the Dakar Education for All (EFA) framework, the UN Millennium Development Goals (MDG) and the Sphere Project's Humanitarian Charter. The CRC, MDG and EFA state the right to quality education for all, including those affected by emergencies. This handbook is a tool to be used in efforts to achieve a minimum level of educational access and provision to fulfil this right.

The Sphere Project's Humanitarian Charter and Minimum Standards in Disaster Response, which was launched in 1997 by a group of humanitarian NGOs and the Red Cross and Red Crescent movement, articulate what people affected by disasters have a right to expect from humanitarian assistance. The Sphere handbook includes the Humanitarian Charter and minimum standards for the core sectors of water supply and sanitation; food security, nutrition and food aid; shelter and site management; and health services. It does not address education services.

The Humanitarian Charter is based on the principles and provisions of international humanitarian law, international human rights law, refugee law and the Code of Conduct for the International Red Cross and Red Crescent Movement and Non-Governmental Organisations (NGOs) in Disaster Relief. The Charter describes the core principles that govern humanitarian action and reasserts the right of populations affected by emergencies to protection and assistance. It also reasserts the right of disaster-affected populations to life with dignity. The Charter points out the legal responsibilities of states and warring parties to guarantee the right to protection and assistance. When the relevant authorities are unable and/or unwilling to fulfil their responsibilities, they are obliged to allow humanitarian organisations to provide humanitarian protection and assistance (www.sphereproject.org).

When to use the INEE Minimum Standards

The Minimum Standards for Education in Emergencies, Chronic Crises and Early Reconstruction are designed for use in emergency response, and may also be useful in emergency preparedness and in humanitarian advocacy. They are applicable in a wide range of situations, including natural disasters and armed conflicts. In this handbook, 'emergency' is used as a generic term to cover two broad categories: 'natural disasters' and 'complex emergencies', which are defined below.

- *Natural disasters* include, among others, hurricanes/typhoons, earthquakes, droughts and floods. Some natural disasters, such as earthquakes, can occur without warning, and have a major impact on those living in the vicinity. Others, such as drought, may develop more slowly but have an equally devastating impact.

[1] Definitions adapted from the International Save the Children Allliance, 2001.

- *Complex emergencies* are situations that are 'man-made' and are often caused by conflict or civil unrest, which may be compounded by a natural disaster. In such circumstances, the lives, safety, well-being and dignity of the populations concerned are endangered by various crisis factors, such as natural and man-made disasters and armed conflict.

The information contained in this handbook is not prescriptive. The minimum standards have been developed by stakeholders from a variety of levels (e.g. households and communities, local authorities, ministry officials, funding agencies, implementers, etc.) and have evolved out of emergency and early reconstruction environments around the world. The standards provide guidance on how national governments, other authorities, and national and international agencies may respond and establish education programmes in emergency settings. The standards are designed to be used by communities, governments, other authorities and humanitarian workers to meet education needs, as defined by the immediate populace.

Timeframe

The timeframe in which the minimum standards are used depends largely on the context. They are applicable in a wide range of emergency settings, from early response in emergencies to early reconstruction stages, and may be used by a diverse audience. Indicators in this handbook are not universally applicable to every situation, nor to every potential user. It may take weeks, months or even years to achieve some of the standards and indicators specified. In some cases the minimum standards and indicators may be achieved without the need for external assistance; in other cases it may be necessary for education authorities and agencies to collaborate to achieve them. When applying these standards and indicators, it is important that all relevant actors agree on a timeframe for implementation and for achieving results.

How to use the Minimum Standards

There are many manuals and toolkits designed by international agencies and NGOs that provide practical guidance to educational workers in emergencies and early reconstruction efforts, dealing with various aspects of learning and psychosocial activities. These same organisations, as well as ministries of education and other education officials, have developed guides and policies on establishing and maintaining quality education programmes. This handbook does not provide a detailed description of strategies and programmes to design and implement in the field. However, it offers a set of minimum standards, key indicators and guidance notes that inform humanitarian action in the context of education, from the development of education programmes to their implementation and continuity, as well as government and community support. The minimum standards are presented in five categories. These are:

- **Minimum standards common to all categories:** this section focuses on the essential areas of community participation and the use of local resources when applying the standards contained in this handbook, as well as ensuring that emergency education responses are based on an initial assessment that is followed by an appropriate response and continued monitoring and evaluation;

- **Access and learning environment:** focuses on partnerships to promote access to learning opportunities and inter-sectoral linkages with, for example, health, water and sanitation, food aid/nutrition and shelter, to enhance security and physical, cognitive and psychological well-being;

- **Teaching and learning:** focuses on critical elements that promote effective teaching and learning: 1) curriculum, 2) training, 3) instruction and 4) assessment;

- **Teachers and other education personnel:** focuses on the administration and management of human resources in the field of education, including recruitment and selection, conditions of service, and supervision and support; and

- **Education policy and coordination:** focuses on policy formulation and enactment, planning and implementation, and coordination.

The difference between standards and indicators

The *minimum standards* are based on the principle that affected populations have the right to life with dignity. They articulate the minimum level of educational access and provision to be attained in a situation of humanitarian assistance. They are qualitative in nature and are meant to be universal and applicable in any environment. The *key indicators* for each standard are signals that show whether the standard has been attained. They function as tools to measure and communicate the impact (or result) of programmes as well as the process (or methods) used, whether qualitative or quantitative. Without the key indicators, the minimum standards would be little more than statements of good intent, difficult to put into practice. The *guidance notes* in each chapter relate to specific points that should be considered when applying the standards in different situations. They offer advice on priority issues and on tackling practical difficulties, and may also describe dilemmas, controversies or gaps in current knowledge. Guidance notes relate to specific key indicators, and the link is signalled in the text. Key indicators should always be read in conjunction with the relevant guidance note(s).

It is important to remember that all the sections are interconnected, and that frequently standards described in one section need to be addressed in conjunction with standards described in others. Where appropriate, guidance notes identify linkages to other relevant standards, indicators or guidance notes.

Cross-cutting issues

In the development of the minimum standards, care has been taken to address several important issues. These relate to human and children's rights, gender, the right of the population to participate, HIV/AIDS, disability and vulnerability. These elements have been incorporated into the relevant standards rather than being dealt with in a separate section.

Scope and limitations

The standards for the different sections do not stand alone: they are interdependent. However, there is inevitably a tension between the formulation of universal standards and the ability to apply them in practice. Every context is different. For this reason, the global development process used to formulate the standards ensured a wide and broad-based participation of humanitarian workers, educators, governments, education authorities, civil society actors and affected people from different regional, country and local contexts.

In some instances, local factors may make the realisation of the minimum standards and key indicators unattainable. When this is the case, the gap between the standards and indicators listed in the handbook and the ones reached in actual practice must be described, and the reasons for the gap, and what needs to be changed in order to realise the standards, must be explained.

The INEE Minimum Standards will not solve all of the problems of educational response; however, they do offer a tool for humanitarian agencies, governments and local populations to enhance the effectiveness and quality of their educational assistance, and thus to make a significant difference in the lives of people affected by disaster.

1.

Minimum Standards Common to All Categories

Introduction

This section details six core process standards that are integral to each of the other categories in this handbook. The standards are: 1) community participation, 2) local resources, 3) initial assessment, 4) response strategy, 5) monitoring and 6) evaluation. They are presented in two sub-groups, under the headings Community Participation (participation and resources) and Analysis (assessment, response, monitoring and evaluation). By implementing the standards described here, humanitarian actors and community members will support the realisation of the standards in the areas of Access and Learning Environment, Teaching and Learning, Teachers and Other Education Personnel, and Education Policy and Coordination.

Links to international legal instruments

Everyone has the right to life with dignity and respect for their human rights, including the right to education. Humanitarian actors have the responsibility to provide assistance in a manner that is consistent with human rights, including the right to participation, non-discrimination and information, as reflected in the body of international human rights, humanitarian and refugee law. In the Sphere Project's Humanitarian Charter and the *Code of Conduct for the International Red Cross and Red Crescent Movement and Non-Governmental Organisations in Disaster Relief*, humanitarian agencies undertake to make themselves accountable to those they seek to assist. The common standards outline the responsibilities of organisations and individuals when providing education assistance.

The importance of the standards common to all categories

It is critical that this section involving community participation and analysis be read first, before turning to the relevant technical section, as the standards outlined here make up an overarching system that embodies all the minimum standards. The collection and analysis of educational data are important in all stages of an emergency. At the beginning of a crisis, resources, needs and gaps must be identified in order to design programmes and direct resources appropriately.

Effective emergency education programmes that meet the needs of disaster-affected populations must be based on a clear understanding of the context. Initial assessments will analyse the nature of the emergency and its effect on a population. The capacities of affected people and available local resources should be identified, at the same time as assessing their needs and vulnerabilities and any gaps in essential services. To ensure the effectiveness of programmes, emergency education assessments must include the participation of not only the emergency-affected community but also the local government and humanitarian actors working on education and non-education issues. Assessments must also consider both formal and non-formal education for all sections of the population. Education cannot be considered in isolation from other sectors, or in isolation from economics, religious and traditional beliefs, social practices, political and security factors, coping mechanisms or anticipated future developments. Analysis of the causes and effects of the emergency is critical. If the problem is not correctly identified and understood then it will be difficult, if not impossible, to respond appropriately.

Response depends on a number of factors, including actors' capacity, area(s) of expertise, budget constraints, familiarity with the region or situation, and security risks for staff and learners. The response standards detailed here are designed to clarify 'who does what when'. Once an appropriate response has been determined, targeting mechanisms should be established that enable actors to provide assistance impartially and without discrimination, according to need.

Monitoring systems to collect and analyse information should be established early in the process to continually measure progress against objectives and to check on the continuing relevance of the programme within an evolving context. Evaluations, which may be carried out during or at the end of the response, should take place at regular intervals depending on the duration of the programme, and should determine the overall effectiveness of the programme, identifying lessons that may improve similar programmes in the future. Relevant stakeholders and learners should be actively involved in the evaluation process. The processes, contents and outcomes of monitoring and evaluation should be transparent and widely disseminated to beneficiaries and other stakeholders, without compromising the security of those involved. In some situations, information is politically or socio-culturally sensitive; therefore, collected data and information must be handled with discretion.

Effective emergency education programmes are based on a thorough understanding of the crisis-affected community and its active involvement in the design of the programme. The term 'community participation' refers to both the processes and activities that allow members of an affected population to be heard, empowering them to be part of decision-making processes and enabling them to take direct action on education issues. There are various degrees or levels of participation – symbolic/token participation, consultation and full participation. While full participation is often difficult to achieve in the emergency circumstances in which we work, consultation is the minimum target for education in emergencies, and all-inclusive, full participation is the goal.

Experience has shown that token participation is a missed opportunity and is ineffective in the provision of quality and lasting programmes. The participation of emergency-affected community members – including vulnerable groups – in the assessment, planning, implementation, management and monitoring of responses should be maximised to ensure the appropriateness, effectiveness and quality of disaster response. Active involvement of the community facilitates the identification of community-specific education issues and the strategies that are effective in addressing them. Additionally, community participation serves as a strategy to identify and mobilise local resources within a community, as well as build consensus and support for education programmes. Community participation must include real and sustained empowerment and capacity building, and must build upon efforts already under way on the ground.

Systematic sharing of knowledge and information among all those involved in response is fundamental to achieving both a common understanding of problems and effective coordination among agencies. Standardised systems and methods of collecting and analysing data should be promoted. This will enable information to be easily documented, shared and disseminated.

Minimum standards: these are qualitative in nature and specify the minimum levels to be attained in the provision of education response.

Key indicators: these are 'signals' that show whether the standard has been attained. They provide a way of measuring and communicating the impact, or result, of programmes as well as the process, or methods, used. The indicators may be qualitative or quantitative.

Guidance notes: these include specific points to consider when applying the standard and indicators in different situations, guidance on tackling practical difficulties, and advice on priority issues. They may also include critical issues relating to the standard or indicators, and describe dilemmas, controversies or gaps in current knowledge. Annex 2 includes a select list of references, which point to sources of information on both general issues and specific technical issues relating to this section.

Community Participation

Standard 1
Participation

Emergency-affected community members actively participate in assessing, planning, implementing, monitoring and evaluating the education programme.

Standard 2
Resources

Local community resources are identified, mobilised and used to implement education programmes and other learning activities.

Annex 2: References and Resource Guide
Community Participation section

Community participation standard 1: participation

Emergency-affected community members actively participate in assessing, planning, implementing, monitoring and evaluating the education programme.

Key indicators (to be read in conjunction with the guidance notes)

- The emergency-affected community, through its chosen representatives, is involved in prioritising and planning education activities to ensure effective delivery of the education programme (see guidance notes 1-5).

- Children and youth are involved in the development and implementation of education activities (see guidance note 6).

- The community education committee holds public meetings to conduct social audits of education activities and their budgets (see guidance note 7).

- Training and capacity-building opportunities exist for community members, including children and youth, to manage education activities (see guidance note 8).

Guidance notes

1. *Community representation in education programmes:* throughout the minimum standards, the term 'community education committee' refers to a committee established to identify and address the educational needs of a community, with representatives drawn from parents and/or parent-teacher associations, local agencies, civil society associations, community organisations and youth and women's groups, among others, as well as teachers and learners (where appropriate). A community education committee may have sub-committees whose members are represented in its composition. In some cases, community education committees will be responsible for a single education programme and in others for several education programmes in a particular location.

   Family, community and school linkages are strengthened in emergency situations through the involvement of parents/guardians in the development and management of the learning environment. Structures for family, community and school linkages should be developed in a participatory, consultative manner. This applies to the development of community education committees, parent-teacher associations, etc., as well as to special measures needed to cope with local circumstances and problems (e.g. child-headed households). A community-based approach will help to create structures (if they are not already in place) and strengthen existing structures that respect local culture and educational traditions and draw on local coping mechanisms.

2. *Community education committees:* representation should be inclusive, with the participation of groups and institutions such as local NGOs, religious institutions,

traditional leaders, groups with special educational needs, marginalised groups, women and girls, clans, tribes, age groups, etc. Representatives should be selected through a democratic process. During the reconstruction phase, the community education committee should be statutorily recognised and legally registered to act as an official institution/organisation. Where community education committees with similar functions and responsibilities already exist, they should be adapted to avoid setting up parallel institutions.

The community education committee should be inclusive and balanced and should reflect the diversity of the affected population including, but not limited to, gender, age, ethnic and religious groups and social categories. It is important to support women and girls in becoming equal partners in development by increasing and ensuring equity with regard to their participation in community education committees.

3. *Roles and responsibilities* of community education committee members should be clearly defined and readily available to the community. These may include, but not be limited to, the following:
   - meeting regularly to discuss issues of concern and to make decisions;
   - keeping minutes of meetings, decisions and community financial and in-kind contributions;
   - providing culturally appropriate approaches (e.g. flexible school calendars, education programme curricula that reflect the community context and involve community members, etc.); and
   - communicating with the community, education programme and/or national and local authorities to promote good relationships between the education programme and community members.

4. *Community involvement in designing education responses:* all governmental and non-governmental agencies should agree upon and establish procedures for ensuring community participation in designing education responses. These procedures should be an essential part of the immediate response from day one, and should include the use of participatory methodologies to rapidly establish:
   - the immediate education needs of diverse sub-groups (children, youth and adults);
   - available human capacity and time, as well as financial and material resources;
   - power dynamics between sub-groups, including language groups;
   - security limitations;
   - safe locations for education provision; and
   - strategies for integrating relevant life-saving educational messages into all aspects of emergency relief.
   (See also Analysis standard 2, guidance note 5 on page 24, Analysis standard 3 on page 25 and Education policy and coordination standard 2 on page 76).

5. *Local education action plan:* the community and the community education committee may prioritise and plan education activities through a participatory grass-roots planning process that reflects the needs, concerns and values of the emergency-affected people, particularly those belonging to vulnerable groups. The result of this planning process is a community-based education action plan. This plan provides a framework for improving

the quality of formal and/or non-formal education services and programmes.

An education action plan may have several objectives, including but not limited to:
- developing a shared vision among actors of what the learning environment might become, articulated through activities, indicators and targets;
- gaining agreement and shared commitment among actors on priorities for improving specific conditions in the learning environment; and
- articulating a plan of action with specific tasks and responsibilities that various stakeholders are to fulfil within given time periods, in order to accomplish targets outlined in the plan.

Local education action plans should define the collaborative roles of all stakeholders, including supporting agencies, community education committees and education programme stakeholders. Action plans should also incorporate a code of conduct to ensure regular community monitoring and assessment and help to establish a culture of involvement to sustain broad community participation. This may include areas such as planning, child protection, promoting the participation of girls and women and persons from vulnerable groups, implementation of teaching and learning activities, supervision, monitoring, resource mobilisation, recruitment and training of staff, infrastructure maintenance and development, coordination with relevant external agencies, and integration with health, hygiene, nutrition, water supply and sanitation interventions, where appropriate. It is important that all community members have access to information so that they can advise their community education committee how to effectively manage the education programme (see also Teachers and other education personnel standard 2 on page 67 and Education policy and coordination standard 3 on page 77).

6. *Children's participation in education activities:* Article 13 of the United Nations Convention on the Rights of the Child (CRC) gives children the right to have a say in matters affecting their own lives, to prepare for their responsibilities in adulthood. This article is applicable to all children in all emergency situations, including chronic crises and early reconstruction.

Learners, especially youth and adults, should be involved in the development and management of the system providing their education. Children must be trained in practices that help protect themselves and other children in their community. Training should emphasise their capacity to participate constructively and initiate positive change, e.g. suggesting improvements in school activities or reporting and preventing abuse within the learning environment (see also Access and learning environment standard 2 on page 45 and Teachers and other education personnel standard 3 on page 69).

Tasks which arise during emergencies (e.g. providing recreational activities for children and youth) can be used to involve young people, especially those not attending schools, in activities that are important for the community. This gives them positive alternatives in the face of negative influences such as crime, armed groups, etc.

7. *Social audits* are community-based evaluations of the education programme. They should be conducted to assess its human, financial and material inputs, identify what is still needed and what is actually available, and monitor the effectiveness of the programme, among other aspects.

   It may not always be possible to conduct social audits during the onset or mid-term stages of an emergency. However, once an emergency has stabilised (e.g. long-term chronic crisis or early reconstruction stages), social audits provide communities with an opportunity to build their capacity to more effectively monitor their education programmes (see also Analysis standard 4 on page 27).

8. *Capacity building:* it is not realistic to expect community members to have the technical capability to manage and own education activities without adequate and appropriate training and mentoring. Training programmes should assess community capacity and identify training needs and ways to address these needs. In addition to capacity building for members of the community education committee, education programmes should involve community members in the work of education programmes and provide training, in order to promote the quality and sustainability of their support.

Community participation standard 2: resources

Local community resources are identified, mobilised and used to implement education programmes and other learning opportunities.

Key indicators (to be read in conjunction with the guidance notes)

- Communities, education personnel and learners identify education resources in the community (see guidance note 1).

- Community resources are mobilised to strengthen access to education, protection and the quality of the education programme (see guidance notes 2-3).

- Stakeholders recognise and support the capacity of communities, and education programming is designed to maximise the use of local skills and capacities (see guidance notes 4-5).

Guidance notes

1. *Community resources* include human, intellectual, monetary or material resources existing in the community. Resource mobilisation should be linked to improving the quality of the learning environment. This may include the physical environment (e.g. material and labour contributions to school construction, maintenance and repairs) and the mental and emotional environment (e.g. psychosocial support for students and teachers/facilitators, or addressing protection issues). Records should be kept to promote transparency and accountability (see also Access and learning environment standards 2-3 on pages 45-48).

2. *Promoting access and security:* community members should be mobilised to devote time and resources to helping children in vulnerable groups enrol in school and attend regularly, e.g. through initiatives by women's and youth groups to provide decent clothing for children from the poorest families, or to provide food to child-headed families. Women can support the participation of girls in school by serving as classroom assistants, providing security from harassment, and community members can contribute their time by escorting children to and from school, where necessary (see also Access and learning environment standards 2-3 on pages 45-48).

3. *Building sustainability:* communities should be provided with training in roles and responsibilities in managing the learning environment, resource mobilisation and management, and sustainability (e.g. maintenance of facilities, special measures to ensure participation of vulnerable students, etc.) over the longer term.

4. *Recognition of community contributions:* reporting to donors should incorporate quantitative and qualitative information on the contribution of communities. A strong community contribution may be seen as indicative of commitment and likely sustainability of programmes.

5. *Local capacity:* participation in the intervention should reinforce people's sense of dignity and hope in times of crisis. Programmes should be designed to build upon local capacity and avoid undermining people's own coping strategies.

Analysis

Standard 1
Initial assessment

A timely education assessment of the emergency situation is conducted in a holistic and participatory manner.

Standard 2
Response strategy

A framework for an education response is developed, including a clear description of the problem and a documented strategy for action.

Standard 3
Monitoring

All relevant stakeholders regularly monitor the activities of the education response and the evolving education needs of the affected population.

Standard 4
Evaluation

There is a systematic and impartial evaluation of the education response in order to improve practice and enhance accountability.

Appendix 1
Assessment Framework

Appendix 2
Planning in an Emergency: Situation Analysis Checklist

Appendix 3
Information Gathering and Needs Assessment Form

Annex 2: References and Resource Guide
Analysis section

Analysis standard 1: initial assessment

A timely education assessment of the emergency situation is conducted in a holistic and participatory manner.

Key indicators (to be read in conjunction with the guidance notes)

- An initial rapid education assessment is undertaken as soon as possible, taking into account security and safety (see guidance notes 1-3).

- Core stakeholders are involved in identifying what data need to be collected; in the development, interpretation and refinement of indicators; and in information management and dissemination (see guidance notes 4-5).

- A comprehensive assessment of education needs and resources for the different levels and types of education, and for all emergency-affected locations, is undertaken with the participation of core stakeholders, and updated on a regular basis (see guidance note 4).

- Education is part of an inter-sectoral assessment that collects data on the political, social, economic and security environment; demographics; and available resources, to determine what services are required for the affected population (see guidance note 6).

- The assessment analyses existing and potential threats to the protection of learners, using a structured risk assessment of threats, vulnerabilities and capacities (see guidance note 7).

- Local capacities, resources and strategies for learning and education are identified, both prior to and during the emergency.

- The assessment identifies local perceptions of the purpose and relevance of education and of priority educational needs and activities.

- A system is established for sharing assessment findings and storing education data (see guidance note 8).

Guidance notes

1. *The timing of assessments* should take into consideration the security and safety of the assessment team and the affected population. Where access is limited, alternative strategies should be explored, such as secondary sources, local leadership and community networks. When greater access is possible, the first assessment should be upgraded and based on more extensive data and information collected. The assessment should be updated regularly (at least quarterly), drawing on monitoring and evaluation data, review of programme achievements and constraints, and information on unmet needs.

2. *Assessment data and information collection* should be planned and conducted to understand educational needs, capacities, resources and gaps. An overall assessment, covering all types of education and all locations, should be completed as soon as

possible, but this should not delay the speedy preparation of partial assessments to inform immediate action. Field visits by different education providers should be coordinated, where possible, to avoid a continuous stream of visitors distracting staff from the emergency response.

Qualitative and quantitative assessment tools should be consistent with international standards, EFA goals and rights-based guidelines. This helps to connect global initiatives with the local community and promote linkages at the local level to global frameworks and indicators. Data collection forms should be standardised in-country to facilitate the coordination of projects at an inter-agency level and minimise the demands on information suppliers. The forms should provide space for additional information deemed important by the local/community respondents.

Ethical considerations are essential to any form of data collection in a humanitarian response. Collecting information for any purpose, including monitoring, assessment or surveys, can put people at risk – not only because of the sensitive nature of the information collected, but also because simply participating in the process may cause people to be targeted or put at risk. The basic principles of respect, do no harm, and non-discrimination must be kept in mind and those collecting the information have responsibility to protect and inform participants of their rights. See Analysis references in Annex 2 (on page 86) for a link to the document *Making Protection A Priority: A Guidebook for Incorporating Protection into Data Collection in Humanitarian Assistance.*

3. *Methods of analysis:* in order to minimise bias, data should be triangulated from multiple sources during analysis, before conclusions are drawn. Triangulation is a mixed-method approach to collecting and analysing data to measure overlapping but also different facets of a phenomenon, yielding an enriched understanding to ensure the validity of qualitative data. Local perceptions are also included in the analysis, to avoid a humanitarian response based solely on outside perceptions and priorities.

4. *Stakeholders should include* as many individuals as possible from the affected population group(s). Stakeholder participation in data and information collection, analysis, and information management and dissemination may be limited by circumstances during the initial assessment, but should be increased during later assessments and monitoring and evaluation.

5. *Assessment findings* should be made available as soon as possible so that activities can be planned. Pre-crisis data and post-crisis assessments that identify education needs and resources (e.g. by authorities, NGOs, specialised agencies within the humanitarian community, and the local community) should be made readily available to all actors. This is particularly useful if actors cannot access the location during an emergency.

6. *General emergency assessments* should include an education or child protection specialist on the emergency team to collect data on education and child protection needs and resources. Agencies should commit resources and build staff and organisational capacity to carry out these activities.

7. *Risk analysis:* it is important to consider all aspects of the situation that may affect the health and safety of children and youth, in so far as education may constitute a protective and/or risk factor. The assessment should include a list or table of risks (a 'risk matrix'), which should document for different age groups and vulnerable groups the risks associated with factors such as natural disasters and environmental hazards; landmines or unexploded ordnance; safety of buildings and other infrastructure; child protection and security; threats to mental and physical health; problems regarding teachers' qualifications, school enrolment and curricula; and other relevant information (for a sample risk matrix, see the MSEE CD-ROM).

The assessment should state the risk management strategies needed for prevention, mitigation and action related to emergencies (preparedness, response, reconstruction and rehabilitation) during adverse events of a natural or provoked nature. This may in some circumstances require each educational centre to have a school contingency and security plan to prevent and respond to emergencies. Where necessary, each educational centre should prepare a risk map showing its potential threats and highlighting the factors that affect its vulnerability.

8. *Sharing assessment findings:* this should be coordinated by the relevant authorities at the local or national level. If there are no competent authorities or organisations to do this, an international lead actor, such as the United Nations Office for the Coordination of Humanitarian Affairs (OCHA), should be named to head up the mechanism for coordinating and sharing information. The sharing of assessment findings should lead to the prompt introduction of a statistical framework and the output of data that can be used by all stakeholders (see also Education policy and coordination standard 3 on page 77).

Analysis standard 2: response strategy

A framework for an education response is developed, including a clear description of the problem and a documented strategy for action.

Key indicators (to be read in conjunction with the guidance notes)

- Baseline data are collected systematically at the start of a programme.

- Emergency education response strategies reflect a clear understanding of the overall data (see guidance notes 1-2).

- Valid benchmarks and indicators are identified to monitor the impacts of the educational response on children, youth and the whole community.

- Information collected from the initial assessment is updated with new data that inform ongoing programme development (see guidance note 3).

- Education response strategies prioritise the safety and well-being of all children and youth, including those who are vulnerable or have special education needs.

- Education response strategies progressively meet the needs of emergency-affected populations for inclusive and quality education, and serve to strengthen national education programmes (see guidance notes 4-6).

Guidance notes

1. *Proposals for response* should ensure that essential activities are budgeted for, with adequate funding to meet the minimum standards described here. Proposals should indicate which education activities are envisaged at which locations, estimating the degree of coverage for assessed needs for different levels and types of education and indicating whether other organisations are known to be committed to meeting the remaining needs. There should be as much flexibility as possible to respond to the actual demand for education, if greater than foreseen. Efforts should be made to promote sustainability and harmonisation between organisations when setting levels and types of emergency education expenditure (e.g. on remuneration, equipment etc.).

2. *Capacity building for data collection and analysis:* proposals should include capacity building of staff, in particular national staff, for baseline data collection and analysis and to carry out the tasks of monitoring and evaluation. These are often not taken fully into account during the proposal process.

3. *Updating of strategies:* proposals for response should be reviewed and updated at least quarterly during emergencies and early reconstruction. They should take into account achievements to date, changes in the emergency situation and current estimates of unmet needs. The aim should be for progressive improvements in quality and coverage, as well as longer-term sustainability, when applicable.

4. *Donor response:* donors should regularly review both the quality and coverage of emergency education response, including the enrolment and retention of learners from vulnerable groups. They should ensure access to educational opportunities in the various emergency-affected locations. Funding should be provided so that education for local populations in locations hosting refugees or internally displaced populations meets minimum standards (see also Access and learning environment standard 1, guidance note 8 on page 44).

5. *Strengthening national programmes:* emergency education response, especially for non-displaced populations and during reconstruction, should be planned to harmonise with and strengthen national education programmes, including national and local education planning, administration, management and in-service teacher training and support.

6. *Overcoming constraints of organisational mandates:* assistance organisations with a limited mandate (e.g. mandates limited to children, or to refugees and their successful repatriation) should ensure that their education response is dovetailed with that of government and organisations with a broader mandate, so that all education needs are met. Education strategies for each affected region should cater for early childhood development needs, as well as for the needs of youth, including secondary, higher and

vocational education, pre-service teacher training and appropriate alternative education. Strategies for educational development in areas receiving returnees should include provision for longer-term support of programmes developed with the help of humanitarian organisations that have time constraints on their intervention (e.g. in support of repatriation and initial reintegration of refugees).

Analysis standard 3: monitoring

All relevant stakeholders regularly monitor the activities of the education response and the evolving education needs of the affected population.

Key indicators (to be read in conjunction with the guidance notes)

- Systems for continuous monitoring of emergency situations and interventions are in place and functioning (see guidance notes 1-2).

- Women, men, children and youth from all affected groups are regularly consulted and are involved in monitoring activities (see guidance note 2).

- Education data are systematically and regularly collected, starting with baseline information and following with tracking of subsequent changes and trends (see guidance notes 3-4).

- Personnel are trained in data collection methodologies and analysis to ensure that the data are reliable and the analysis is verifiable and credible (see guidance note 5).

- Education data are analysed and shared with stakeholders at pre-determined regular intervals (see guidance note 3).

- Monitoring systems and databases are regularly updated on the basis of feedback to reflect new trends and to allow for informed decision-making.

- Data that identify changes, new trends, needs and resources are provided to education programme managers on a regular basis.

- Programme adjustments are made, when necessary, as a result of monitoring.

Guidance notes

1. *Monitoring* should reflect the changing educational needs of the population, as well as the extent to which programmes are meeting those needs, in order to be relevant and responsive and to take account of possibilities for improvement. Not all data need to be collected with the same frequency. The design of monitoring therefore will involve decisions as to how often to collect particular types of data, based on need, and the

amount of resources consumed by data collection and processing. Many types of information can be collected from schools and other education programmes on a sample basis, giving quick indications of needs and problems (e.g. data on enrolment, drop-out, whether students eat before attending school, number of textbooks, teaching and learning materials available, etc.). Monitoring of children out of school and their reasons for not enrolling or for non-attendance can also be undertaken through visits to a small sample of households in selected locations, as well as meetings with community groups.

2. *People involved in monitoring:* people who are able to collect information from all groups in the affected population in a culturally acceptable manner should be included, especially with regard to gender and language skills. Local cultural practices may require that women or minority groups be consulted separately by individuals who are culturally acceptable.

3. *Education Management Information Systems (EMIS)* may have been disrupted by the emergency. Basic data collection and simple processing should be restored as a matter of priority, through inter-agency cooperation and support to the national authorities. The development or rehabilitation of a national EMIS may require capacity building and resources at national, regional and local levels to develop, collect, manage, interpret, apply and disseminate available information. This action should be initiated as early as possible in the emergency, with the aim being to have a functioning monitoring system in place by the early reconstruction phase.

A critical component of the EMIS is compatible software. National- and district-level education offices and other education sub-sectors (e.g. national training institutes) should have complementary software to set up compatible databases to facilitate the exchange of information.

4. *Monitoring of learners* should take place whenever possible after they complete or leave a course. Monitoring can cover the retention of literacy and numeracy skills and access to post literacy reading materials. For vocational education, monitoring should keep track of employment opportunities and the use made by ex-trainees of their vocational skills, through follow-up by placement staff as well as tracer studies. Post-programme monitoring provides valuable feedback for programme design (see also Teaching and learning standard 4 on page 62).

5. *Validity of data:* all analyses should have documentation that explains 1) indicator definition, 2) data source, 3) method of collection, 4) data collectors and 5) data analysis procedures. Any anomalies that may have occurred during the administration, collection or analysis of the data should also be noted. Data can be skewed by respondents seeking to maximise resource allocations (e.g. inflated enrolment or attendance figures) or to avoid blame. Staff training should be supplemented by a policy of unannounced monitoring visits to improve the validity of data.

Analysis standard 4: evaluation

There is a systematic and impartial evaluation of the education response in order to improve practice and enhance accountability.

Key indicators (to be read in conjunction with the guidance notes)

- Evaluation of policies, programmes and outcomes of interventions is conducted at appropriate intervals against overall response strategies, specific educational and child protection objectives, and minimum standards (see guidance note 1).

- Information is sought on the unintended effects of the intervention.

- Information is collected in a transparent and impartial manner from all stakeholders, including the affected populations and partners from other sectors.

- All stakeholders, including marginalised groups, community education committees, national and local education officials, teachers and learners, are included in evaluation activities (see guidance note 2).

- Lessons and good practices are widely shared with the broader national and local community and humanitarian community, and are fed into post-emergency advocacy, programmes and policies to contribute to national and global education goals (see guidance note 3).

Guidance notes

1. *Evaluations* should collect both qualitative and quantitative data to develop a holistic picture. Qualitative data provide contextual information and help to explain the statistical data collected. Qualitative data can be collected through interviews, observations and written documents; quantitative data can be collected through surveys and questionnaires.

   Evaluations should provide a comprehensive appraisal of human, material and financial inputs; learner access, retention, inclusion and protection; teaching learning processes; recognition and certification of learning; in-service teacher training; impact on individual learners, including opportunities for further studies and employment; and impact on the wider community.

2. *Capacity building through evaluation:* the evaluation budget should include provision for workshops with stakeholders to introduce evaluation concepts, develop the evaluation framework and processes on a participative basis, and review and interpret findings together. It is particularly beneficial to involve the staff of an education programme in aspects of the evaluation process. This can help them develop the conceptual basis for later 'ownership' and implementation of recommendations. Project beneficiaries, e.g. teachers and other education personnel, can also point out the practical difficulties they face and difficulties that would be encountered as a consequence of particular recommendations.

3. *Sharing findings and lessons learned:* evaluators should be asked to structure their report to include a first section that can be shared in the public domain, with confidential or internal findings presented in a second section that will not be so widely shared.

Minimum Standards Common to all Categories: Appendices

Appendix 1: Assessment Framework

	PROTECTION (physical, legal and material)/HUMAN RIGHTS/RULE OF LAW						
	MORTALITY						
	MORBIDITY			NUTRITIONAL STATUS			
	ACCESS TO POTABLE WATER	ACCESS TO BASIC HEALTH, NUTRITION & PSYCHOSOCIAL SERVICES	FOOD INTAKE	AVAILABILITY AND ADEQUACY OF SHELTER	HEALTHY BEHAVIOURS	LEVELS OF SANITATION	
	FOOD SECURITY			PERFORMANCE OF HEALTH, NUTRITION & PSYCHOSOCIAL SERVICES			
	ECONOMIC & MARKET CONTEXT OF HOUSEHOLDS		EDUCATION	SOCIAL AND CULTURAL CONTEXT		INEQUALITIES	

(Left vertical axis: CAPACITIES and VULNERABILITIES ANALYSIS (e.g. gender, including age and sex disaggregation) PARTICIPATION)

(Right vertical axis: DEMOGRAPHY (Total population, specific vulnerable groups, size of host population, displaced, missing, age and sex distribution, etc.)

NATIONAL CONTEXT	NATIONAL MARKETS
Political, economic, historical, social, government capacity, infrastructure, systems, geography, climate, natural hazards, international organisations, etc.	Functioning (and thereby decreasing need for outside assistance) or dysfunctional?

The Assessment Framework is used as a basis for discussion and analysis, with the objective of reaching a common understanding of the needs of a particular population. This analysis combines evidence and judgment. The Assessment Framework comprises categories, which are issues of concern meriting consideration, not needs per se. While suggesting causality between categories, the framework does not explicitly refer to this, and further elaboration of tools is required to assist assessment teams. Until such tools are developed, teams may choose how to explain causality. The framework provides a more consistent and transparent platform for sharing information with the aim of planning a prioritised humanitarian response to crises. While there is a hierarchy of concerns reflected in each level of the framework, this does not imply a consequent prioritised response. The framework illustrates that different categories are interdependent and should be considered as such. Each category in the framework should be assessed individually (i.e. education) and as part of an integrated assessment (i.e. the impact of the situation in education on other categories in the framework). Protection/human rights/rule of law are overarching issues, which need to be addressed separately and mainstreamed. The starting point for assessment is either geographic or population group.

Source: The Assessment Framework was developed by the Inter-Agency Standing Committee (IASC) CAP Sub-Working Group and refined at a workshop attended by donors, UN agencies, the Red Cross and NGOs, 25 January 2004.

Appendix 2: Planning in an Emergency:
Situation Analysis Checklist

The factors, issues, people and institutions you need to know and understand in order to plan and implement the programme.

1. Baseline Assessment
- What data are required for baseline study?
- What data do you need to plan implementation vs. what is available e.g. school locations (numbers, locations); expected student numbers; teachers numbers; etc.?
- Is there an opportunity to collect baseline data before you start the programme?

2. The Nature of the Situation
- What is the nature of the situation (slow onset or sudden)?
- Are there groups (culture, age, gender, etc.) that are particularly vulnerable or affected by the emergency?

3. The Stability of the Situation
- Is the situation stable (short term/medium term) or still evolving?
- Are there other foreseeable contingencies (a new emergency or a major change to the existing emergency)?
- What factors can be identified that are likely to result in sudden and/or significant changes?

4. The Current Educational System
The Education System
- Is there a functioning education system?
- Is there more than one functioning system within the target population?
- How has the current emergency affected the present education system(s)?
- Are school buildings and infrastructure lacking or destroyed (kitchens, sanitation facilities, storage, etc.)?
- What is the current condition of the learning environment (space, materials, classrooms, staff, etc.)?
- Is the situation the same for boys and girls, or children of different geographic/ethnic/etc. backgrounds?
- Are children enrolled in and regularly attending school? If not, why not?
- Are children affected by hunger while they are at school (e.g. no breakfast, long distance to school, general malnutrition)?
- Are children affected by specific micronutrient deficiencies? Which ones?

Curriculum and Instruction

- Is there a common curriculum?
- Is there a common language (or languages) of instruction?
- Are there teachers, teaching aids and/or learning aids?
- Is there a need for teacher training/retraining?
- Is there a need for informal education and skills training programmes (for demobilised (child) soldiers, out-of-school children and/or other particularly disadvantaged groups)?

5. Key Stakeholders
Identify Key Stakeholders

- Who is doing what?
- Who is responsible for what?
- Who is planning what?
- Who is responsible for what resources?
- Who is responsible for what decisions?
- Other international organisations
- NGOs (international and local)
- Government:
  - What is the current status of the national and local government (legitimacy, interim)?
  - Who administers education?
- Schools (teachers, principals, PTAs)
- Community (leaders, elders, religious, women's associations, health workers, or other community groups)
- Family
  - What is the predominant structure?
  - Has the emergency affected the family structure?
  - Who makes decisions about the children's (in particular girls') participation in education?

6. Available Resources
For Education (see also: 'The Current Educational System' above)

- Are there safe learning spaces?
- Are the available school facilities fully functioning?
- Are there sufficient numbers of teachers and school staff to carry out the day-to-day running of the school?

For Food Aid

- How urgent is it to start food distributions?
- What personnel are available to prepare food?
- What facilities are in place for the preparation of food (school kitchens, storerooms, cooking/eating utensils, cooking fuel, water source)?
- Is it feasible to put facilities in place?
- Is there transportation/delivery/storage infrastructure?
- What food commodities are going to be available? Where and how quickly can they be acquired and delivered to food distribution points?
- Are there any school health programmes to complement/build on?
- Are there currently any donor commitments?
- Are there any potential implementing partners?

7. Current and Potential Constraints

Security
- Are there safe learning spaces?
- Is there safe access to the learning spaces for children, teachers and aid workers?
- Is there a safe place for the preparation and/or distribution of food?
- Is the transport and delivery of food secure?
- Is the food stored securely?

Gender/Ethnic Constraints
- Are there particular constraints/issues for one gender or another?
- Are there particular constraints/issues related to different groups (ethnic, geographic)?

Legitimacy
- Is there a clear government partner for the planning and implementation of activities?
- Does the creation and support of educational activities have the support of political/local leadership powers? If not, why not?
- Are there risks in proceeding without this support?
- Can proceeding without this support be justified?
- Can the partnership be developed?
- Can the programme be designed to develop and/or attract support?

Adapted from: World Food Programme, Planning for School Feeding in the Emergency Setting – Situation Analysis, Designing the Programme, Implementation, 2004. http://www.wfp.org

Appendix 3: Information Gathering and Needs Assessment Questionnaire

Location(s): _____

Nature of emergency:_____

Main problem(s):_____

Are some schools still functioning?

Yes/No	Location(s)	Number of children attending	
		Girls	Boys
_____	_____	_____	_____
_____	_____	_____	_____
_____	_____	_____	_____

1. Main cause(s)and/or manifestation(s) of problem ☑

School buildings have been damaged ☐	Teachers will not work if unpaid ☐
Water on school premises is unsafe/not available ☐	Travelling has become dangerous ☐
Children are unoccupied/out of school ☐	Teachers are enrolled in army ☐
Equipment/materials not available ☐	Some children have been traumatised ☐
Families cannot afford to buy school materials ☐	Some children are disabled ☐
Teachers have left or are afraid ☐	Children are enrolled in the army ☐
Lack of educated adults to replace teachers ☐	

2. Identification of Children Population

	Total	Girls	Boys
Number of children	_____	_____	_____
0-5 year olds	_____%	_____%	_____%
6-13 year olds	_____%	_____%	_____%
14-18 year olds	_____%	_____%	_____%
Residents	_____%	_____%	_____%
In-movers	_____%	_____%	_____%

3. Comparison with Pre-Emergency Situation

	Total			Girls			Boys		
No of children	Less	Same	More	Less	Same	More	Less	Same	More
0-5 year olds	Less	Same	More	Less	Same	More	Less	Same	More
6-13 year olds	Less	Same	More	Less	Same	More	Less	Same	More
14-18 year olds	Less	Same	More	Less	Same	More	Less	Same	More
Residents	Less	Same	More	Less	Same	More	Less	Same	More
In-movers	Less	Same	More	Less	Same	More	Less	Same	More

Explain any major differences in gender

Are there any other significant issues that need to be addressed i.e. a presence of ethnic groups? Explain

4. What is the children's level of education?

	Early childhood education	Primary education	Middle school education (early adolescents)
% of age group population that have completed	_____	_____	_____

5. What is/are the language(s) used by the children?

	Mother tongue	Spoken ☑	Written ☑
Local languages (specify)	_____	☐	☐
	_____	☐	☐
	_____	☐	☐
Other (specify)	_____	☐	☐
	_____	☐	☐
	_____	☐	☐

6a. Do you possess a map of the region on which community buildings (e.g. schools, health centres, churches) are indicated?

6b. If the answer to 6a is no, could you obtain one?

6c. If the answer to 6b is no, indicate how to obtain this information

7. What locations can be used for classes?

	☑	Number of children that can be accommodated
School/classrooms	☐	_____
Rehabilitation centre	☐	_____
Shelter	☐	_____
Outside(shade/tree)	☐	_____
House	☐	_____
Religious buildings	☐	_____
Clinic	☐	_____
Other(specify)	☐	_____

8. Are the following facilities easily accessible?

	On-site ☑	At a distance(metres) ☑	Not accessible ☑
Water source (specify)	☐	☐	☐
Lavatories	☐	☐	☐
Showers	☐	☐	☐
Toilets	☐	☐	☐
Medical facilities	☐	☐	☐
Facilities for the disabled	☐	☐	☐
Electricity	☐	☐	☐

9. How far would children have to travel to attend classes?

	0-25%	26-50%	51-75%	76-100%
(in metres)		(% of the children group)		
500 metres or less	_____	_____	_____	_____
500 to 1000 metres	_____	_____	_____	_____
> 1000 metres	_____	_____	_____	_____
(in miles)				
1/2 mile or less	_____	_____	_____	_____
1/2 to 1 mile	_____	_____	_____	_____
> 1 mile	_____	_____	_____	_____

10. Are children involved in household chores or any other work?

	Girls	Boys
%	_____	_____
Hours per day	_____	_____
Mainly a.m. or p.m.	_____	_____

11. What quantity (approximately) of learning materials are available and required?

(per child)	Available	Required
Textbooks	_____	_____
Subject 1	_____	_____
Subject 2	_____	_____
Subject 3	_____	_____
Slate(s)	_____	_____
Chalk(s)	_____	_____
Ball sponge(s)	_____	_____
Exercise book(s)	_____	_____
Pen(s)/pencil(s)	_____	_____
Pencil eraser(s)	_____	_____
Colour pencil(s)	_____	_____
Others (specify)	_____	_____

12. What is the quantity (approximately) of teaching materials that are available and required?

	Available	Required
(Per classroom)	_____	_____
Guides/manuals	_____	_____
Record books	_____	_____
Blackboard	_____	_____
Chalk box(es)	_____	_____
Wall charts/maps	_____	_____
Pens/pencils	_____	_____
Stationery	_____	_____
Others (specify)	_____	_____
Recreational materials	_____	_____

13. Who is/might be available to teach children?

	No.	Women (%)	Men(%)
Trained teachers	____	____	____
Para-professionals	____	____	____
Professionals from other fields	____	____	____
(e.g. medical/para-medical)	____	____	____
Older children	____	____	____
Community members	____	____	____
NGO members	____	____	____
Volunteers	____	____	____
Other (specify)	____	____	____

14. What adult human resources are available to support teachers?

	No.	Women(%)	Men(%)	Level of education/Qualification
Para-professionals	__	____	____	_____
Professionals from other fields	__	____	____	_____
(e.g. medical/para-medical)	__	____	____	_____
Older children	__	____	____	_____
Community members	__	____	____	_____
NGO members	__	____	____	_____
Volunteers	__	____	____	_____
Others (specify)	__	____	____	_____

15. Are children accompanied?

	% of children group
By their whole family	_____
By at least one parent	_____
By older siblings	_____
By other family members	_____
By volunteers	_____
Alone	_____

16. Who is the household head?

	% of children group
Mother	_____
Father	_____
Other adult (specify)	_____
Other child (elder sister)	_____
Other child (elder brother)	_____
Other (specify)	_____

17. Economic background of the children's family?

	%
Farmers	_____
Artisans	_____
Nomads	_____
Cattle raisers	_____
Other (specify)	_____

18. What are the special messages to be conveyed to children?

Messages on sanitation & hygiene_____

_____

Health messages _____

_____

Messages on potential dangers such as landmines _____

_____

Life skills (specify) _____

_____

Other (specify) _____

_____

19. Presence of functioning key institutions in affected communities (indicate a few names):

Community committees	Universal	Common	Rare	Non-existent
1 _____	☐	☐	☐	☐
2 _____	☐	☐	☐	☐

Education ministry resources	Universal	Common	Rare	Non-existent
1 _____	☐	☐	☐	☐
2 _____	☐	☐	☐	☐

Teacher training institutes	Universal	Common	Rare	Non-existent
1 _____	☐	☐	☐	☐
2 _____	☐	☐	☐	☐

Education-active domestic NGOs	Universal	Common	Rare	Non-existent
1 _____	☐	☐	☐	☐
2 _____	☐	☐	☐	☐

Education-active int'l NGOs	Universal	Common	Rare	Non- existent
1 _____	☐	☐	☐	☐
2 _____	☐	☐	☐	☐

UN agencies	Universal	Common	Rare	Non-existent
1 _____	☐	☐	☐	☐
2 _____	☐	☐	☐	☐

Other (specify)	Universal	Common	Rare	Non-existent
1 _____	☐	☐	☐	☐
2 _____	☐	☐	☐	☐

2.

Access and Learning Environment

Introduction

During times of crisis, access to a vital right and resource – education – is often extremely limited. However, education can play a crucial role in helping the affected population to cope with their situation by gaining additional knowledge and skills for survival and to regain normalcy in their lives. At the same time, it is often more complicated to organise education activities during emergencies, and there is a danger that vulnerable groups in particular will fail to receive the education offered. Governments, communities and humanitarian organisations have a responsibility to ensure that all individuals have access to relevant, quality education opportunities, and that learning environments are secure and promote both protection and the mental, emotional and physical well-being of learners.

Education programmes in emergencies can provide physical, social and cognitive protection to learners, especially children and youth, and to education personnel. However, learners are too often subject to physical or psychological dangers en route to and from school and within the learning environment itself. These problems affect girls and female teachers disproportionately. In providing education services, there is an obligation to ensure that students are safe both coming to and going from school, as well as in the learning environment itself.

A progressive range of formal and non-formal education opportunities should be provided. If formal education is not immediately possible at the onset of an emergency, education programmes should arrange for recreational activities (sports and play); non-formal education activities; catch-up programmes for older children (if necessary); opportunities for youth to maintain and develop their core study skills; and alternative non-formal education or skills training for children, youth and adults who have not started or completed basic education.

Some groups or individuals may have particular difficulties accessing education in an emergency situation. However, no individual should be denied access to education and learning opportunities because of discrimination. Education providers must assess the particular needs of vulnerable groups with special needs, such as the disabled, adolescent girls, children associated with fighting forces (CAFF), abducted children, teenage mothers, etc., to ensure that they benefit from education opportunities. Educational interventions should focus not only on providing formal and non-formal educational services, but also on addressing the obstacles, such as discrimination, school fees and language barriers, that exclude certain groups. In particular, additional opportunities, whether formal, non-formal or vocational, are needed to address the needs of girls and women who have not had access to education or who face obstacles to continuing their education.

Links to the standards common to all categories

The process by which an education response is developed and implemented is critical to its effectiveness. This section should be utilised in conjunction with the standards common to all categories, which cover community participation, local resources, initial assessment, response, monitoring and evaluation. In particular, the participation of disaster-affected people – including vulnerable groups – should be maximised to ensure its appropriateness and quality.

Minimum standards: these are qualitative in nature and specify the minimum levels to be attained in the provision of education response.

Key indicators: these are 'signals' that show whether the standard has been attained. They provide a way of measuring and communicating the impact, or result, of programmes as well as the process, or methods, used. The indicators may be qualitative or quantitative.

Guidance notes: these include specific points to consider when applying the standard and indicators in different situations, guidance on tackling practical difficulties, and advice on priority issues. They may also include critical issues relating to the standard or indicators, and describe dilemmas, controversies or gaps in current knowledge. Annex 2 includes a select list of references, which point to sources of information on both general issues and specific technical issues relating to this section.

Access and Learning Environment

Standard 1
Equal access

All individuals have access to quality and relevant education opportunities.

Standard 2
Protection and well-being

Learning environments are secure, and promote the protection and mental and emotional well-being of learners.

Standard 3
Facilities

Education facilities are conducive to the physical well-being of learners.

Appendix 1
Psychosocial checklist

Appendix 2
School Feeding Programme Checklist

Annex 2: References and Resource Guide
Access and Learning Environment section

Access and learning environment standard 1: equal access

All individuals have access to quality and relevant education opportunities.

Key indicators (to be read in conjunction with the guidance notes)

- No individual is denied access to education and learning opportunities because of discrimination (see guidance notes 1-2).

- Documents or other requirements are not a barrier to enrolment (see guidance note 3).

- A range of formal and non-formal education opportunities is progressively provided to the affected population to fulfil their education need (see guidance notes 4-5).

- Through training and sensitisation, communities become increasingly involved in ensuring the rights of all members to a quality and relevant education (see guidance notes 6-7).

- Sufficient resources are made available by authorities, donors, NGOs, other development partners and communities to ensure continuity and quality of education activities in all phases of the emergency and early reconstruction (see guidance note 8).

- Learners have the opportunity to safely enter or re-enter the formal education system as soon as possible after any disruption caused by the emergency.

- The education programme is recognised by the education authorities of the host country and/or country of origin.

Guidance notes

1. *Discrimination* refers, but is not limited, to obstacles imposed because of poverty, gender, age, nationality, race, ethnicity, religion, language, culture, political affiliation, sexual orientation, socio-economic background, geographic location or special education needs.

   The International Covenant on Economic, Social and Cultural Rights states the following:
   – Article 2 recognises 'the right to education without discrimination of any kind as to race, colour, sex, language, religion, political or other opinion, national or social origin, property, birth or other status';
   – Article 13 recognises the right of everyone to education that 'shall be directed to the full development of the human personality and the sense of its dignity, and shall strengthen the respect for human rights and fundamental freedoms. Education shall enable all persons to participate effectively in a free society, promote understanding, tolerance and friendship among all nations and all racial, ethnic or religious groups, and further the activities of the United Nations for the maintenance of peace'. Article

13 also commits states to recognise that, with a view to achieving the full realisation of this right: 1) primary education shall be compulsory and available free to all; 2) secondary education in its different forms, including technical and vocational secondary education, shall be made generally available and accessible to all by every appropriate means, and in particular by the progressive introduction of free education; 3) basic education shall be encouraged or intensified as far as possible for those persons who have not received or completed the whole period of their primary education.

2. *International instruments and frameworks* declaring the right to education in emergencies should be upheld. These include, but are not limited to:
   - the Dakar World Education Forum Framework for Action, promoting Education For All, which declares as one of its aims that governments must 'meet the needs of education systems affected by conflict, natural calamities and instability, and conduct education programmes in ways that promote mutual understanding, peace and tolerance, and that help to prevent violence and conflict';
   - the Geneva Convention (IV) Relative to the Protection of Civilian Persons in Time of War (Article 50): 'The Occupying Power shall, with the cooperation of the national and local authorities, facilitate the proper working of all institutions devoted to the care and education of children';
   - the United Nations Convention on the Rights of the Child (CRC), which provides a normative framework for the physical, psychosocial and cognitive protection of learning in emergency settings.

3. *Admission and enrolment:* documentation requirements should be flexible and should not require certificates of citizenship, birth or age certificates, identity papers, school reports, etc., since emergency-affected populations may not have these documents. Age limits should not be enforced for emergency-affected children and youth. Second-chance enrolment for drop-outs should be permitted. Special efforts should be made to target and involve the most marginalised and vulnerable learners. Where there are security concerns, documentation and enrolment information should be kept confidential.

4. *Range of education opportunities:* these opportunities should include early childhood, primary and secondary education, higher education, life skills, vocational training, non-formal education (including literacy and numeracy) and accelerated learning opportunities, where appropriate. Any trauma that learners may have experienced as a result of the emergency itself should not be compounded by the loss of access to education.

Flexible time scheduling, including variable school hours and shifts, outreach education programmes, child-care services for teenage mothers, organised peer support for students facing difficulties integrating into classroom settings, and bridging programmes and vacation studies may allow more learners to benefit from educational opportunities. Forcibly mainstreaming older learners into classes for younger children or allowing them to voluntarily join regular classes for younger children can have negative consequences for both younger and older learners and result in inefficient learning by all. Alternative options, such as separate classes for older learners and accelerated courses, should be used when appropriate. Youth representatives, women's groups, other community members and community leaders should be consulted before introducing alternatives to regular school programmes.

Techniques such as 'school mapping' should also be used during and after emergencies to plan for cost-effective access of potential learners in different locations to the full range of education activities in emergency response.

5. *Age groups:* education opportunities should be prioritised by age group (e.g. children and youth) and content (e.g. life-saving information for all in the initial phase of an emergency). As the emergency stabilises, education opportunities can be expanded for all population groups to improve their lives in a range of relevant ways.

6. *'Quality' and 'relevant education':* see Annex 1: Minimum Standards for Education in Emergencies: Terminology on page 79 for definitions of these terms.

7. *Community involvement:* communities should be actively engaged in education processes. This can help address communication gaps, mobilise additional resources, address security concerns and promote participation among marginalised groups (see also Annex 1: Terminology on page 79 and Community participation standards 1-2 on pages 14-19).

8. *Resources:* donors should be flexible and support a range of strategies to ensure continuity of education initiatives, from the early stages of an emergency through reconstruction. National governments have ultimate responsibility to ensure education and may receive funding from a variety of sources. Other donors include the international community (bilaterals and multilaterals), international and indigenous NGOs, local authorities, faith-based organisations, civil society groups and other development partners (see also Analysis standard 2, guidance note 4 on page 24).

The focus of resource planning should be on extending immediate education opportunities, but sustainability, long-term planning (including the possibility that an emergency may be prolonged) and future reconstruction scenarios should also be considered. Collaboration and coordination with concerned authorities can help to ensure stability (see also Education policy and coordination standard 3 on page 77).

Rapid educational response in emergencies requires quick access to funding, e.g. through emergency reserves or start-up funds. Funding during protracted emergencies should be sufficient to support education for children and youth that will permit them to continue their progress through a normal school programme. At the stage of early reconstruction, funding should be provided where needed to strengthen national and local education administration and planning. Donor resources should enable education programmes to resume in all locations through the use of temporary shelter and the provision of teaching and learning materials.

Access and learning environment standard 2: protection and well-being

Learning environments are secure, and promote the protection and mental and emotional well-being of learners.

Key indicators (to be read in conjunction with the guidance notes)

- Schools and other learning environments are located in close proximity to the populations they serve (see guidance notes 1-2).

- Access routes to the learning environment are safe and secure for all (see guidance note 3).

- The learning environment is free from dangers that may cause harm to learners (see guidance notes 4-5).

- Training programmes for teachers, learners and the community are in place to promote safety, security and protection.

- Teachers and other education personnel are provided with the skills to give psychosocial support to promote learners' emotional well-being (see guidance note 6).

- The community is involved in decisions concerning the location of the learning environment, and in establishing systems and policies to ensure that learners are safe and secure.

- The nutrition and short-term hunger needs of learners are addressed to allow for effective learning to take place at the learning site (see guidance note 7).

Guidance notes

1. *Proximity* should be defined according to local/national standards, taking account of any security problems or other safety concerns. Where distances are considerable, subsidiary (or 'satellite' or 'feeder') classes should be encouraged on sites nearer to their homes for those unable to travel any distance, such as younger children or adolescent girls.

2. *Security:* if the usual education premises are not available or insecure, then alternative sites should be selected which are safe and secure. Schools should not be used as temporary shelters by security forces.

3. *Access routes:* the state has the obligation to ensure security, and this security can relate to sufficient and good-quality policing and the deployment of troops, where appropriate and necessary. In order to enhance this protection and ensure that access routes are safe and secure for all learners and education personnel (regardless of gender, age, nationality, race, ethnicity or physical ability), communities should discuss and agree on proactive measures, such as adult escorts. This can also be part of the community education committee agenda.

4. *Protection:* learners should be protected from dangers that may harm them, including but not limited to: natural hazards, arms, ammunition, landmines, unexploded ordnance, armed personnel, crossfire locations, political and military threats, and recruitment.

Students, especially minorities and girls, often become targets for abuse, violence, recruitment or abduction when going to and from school. In these cases students' security can be improved by a combination of community information campaigns and by having adults from the community escort them. In areas where students must walk back from school at night along poorly lit roads, their clothes or bags should have reflectors or reflective tape attached, or flashlight escorts should be arranged. When and where possible, women should be present on educational premises to reassure female learners. In addition, education programmes should include monitoring of the level of harassment experienced by girls and women.

5. *Non-violent classroom management:* intimidation includes, among other aspects, mental stress, violence, abuse and discrimination. Teachers should receive training in methods of positive classroom management to ensure intimidation does not occur. Corporal punishment should not be used or promoted.

6. *Well-being:* emotional and mental well-being should be understood in the full sense of what is good for a person: security, protection, quality of service, happiness and warmth in the relations between education providers and learners. The activities used to ensure learners' well-being should focus on enhancing sound cognitive development, solid social interactions and good health. Ensuring well-being also contributes to learners' successful completion of a formal or non-formal education programme (see Appendix 1 on page 49 for a Psychosocial Checklist).

7. *Nutrition:* nutritional and short-term hunger needs should be addressed through school feeding programmes or other food security programmes outside the learning environment. If school feeding programmes are implemented, they should follow recognised guidelines used by other agencies, e.g. the World Food Programme (see Appendix 2 on page 51 for a School Feeding Programme Checklist).

Access and learning environment standard 3: facilities

Education facilities are conducive to the physical well-being of learners.

Key indicators (to be read in conjunction with the guidance notes)

- The learning structure and site are accessible to all, regardless of physical ability.

- The learning environment is marked by visible boundaries and clear signs, as appropriate.

- The physical structure used for the learning site is appropriate for the situation and includes adequate space for classes and administration, recreation and sanitation facilities (see guidance note 1).

- Class space and seating arrangements are in line with an agreed ratio of space per learner and teacher, as well as grade level, in order to promote participatory methodologies and learner-centred approaches (see guidance note 1).

- Communities participate in the construction and maintenance of the learning environment (see guidance note 2).

- Basic health and hygiene are promoted in the learning environment.

- Adequate sanitation facilities are provided, taking account of age, gender and special education needs and considerations, including access for persons with disabilities (see guidance note 3).

- Adequate quantities of safe drinking water and water for personal hygiene are available at the learning site (see guidance note 4).

Guidance notes

1. *Structure:* appropriateness of the physical structure should take into account its long-term use (post-emergency), the available budget, community involvement and whether it can be maintained by local authorities and/or the local community at a reasonable cost. The structure may be temporary, semi-permanent, permanent, an extension or mobile.

   The following elements should be kept in mind:
   – locally procured materials and labour, when available, should be used to build the structure. Steps should be taken to ensure that structures are cost-effective and that physical features (e.g. roofs, floors) are durable;
   – adequate lighting, cross-ventilation and heating (wherever required) should be available to promote a quality teaching and learning environment;
   – a locally realistic standard should be set for maximum class size, and every effort should be made to provide enough space for additional classrooms if enrolment

increases, to enable progressive reduction in the use of multiple shifts;

– education programmes need not wait until all of the infrastructure components and adequate space mentioned above are secured. These components, however, should be supplied or adhered to as rapidly as possible.

(See Linkages to Sphere Standards annex on the MSEE CD-ROM for the relevant Sphere shelter standards.)

2. *Maintenance of the learning environment* should include facilities (e.g. latrines, water pumps, etc.) and furniture (e.g. desks, chairs, blackboards, cabinets, etc.).

3. *Sanitation facilities* should include solid waste disposal (containers, waste pits), drainage (soak pits, drainage channels) and adequate water for personal hygiene and to clean latrines/toilets. Learning environments should have separate toilets for males and females and adequate privacy. Sanitary materials should be available for females (see Linkages to Sphere Standards annex on the MSEE CD-ROM for the relevant Sphere standards on excreta disposal and clothing).

4. *Water* should be available within or in close proximity to the learning environment as per local/international standards (see Linkages to Sphere Standards annex on the MSEE CD-ROM for the relevant Sphere water standards).

Access and Learning Environment: Appendices

Appendix 1: Psychosocial Checklist

Specific survey methods will depend on the local situation and culture. The following represents the type of information useful for addressing issues of psychosocial well-being and recovery.

General Conditions
- Were situations of violation of child rights at the origin of traumatic events?
- Have situations of abuse stopped or are they continuing to create a climate of insecurity for children and their families?
- Are families living together?
- Do they have sufficient privacy?
- What is being done to enable families to live in dignity and provide care and protection for their children? What more can be done?
- What are the normal activities in the community to assist children who have difficulties?
- What are the community's normal mechanisms to respond to and deal with psychosocial distress? How can they be strengthened and built on?
- How do the general living arrangements and social organisation of the population affect the protection and care of children?
- What measures could be implemented to improve the living conditions of children and their families?
- Are there persons in the community who could provide regular activities for children, such as non-formal education, play and recreation?

Parents
- What is the nature of hardship and stress faced by parents that is affecting their well-being as well as how they care for their children?
- What measures can be implemented to reduce this hardship?
- Are parents seen beating their children more than is normally permissible within their cultural framework?
- Are there opportunities in place for parents to discuss and seek support for distressing difficulties that they and their children must deal with?

Children
- Are children being provided with inadequate nurture and care?
- What measures might be taken to improve the care that such children receive?
- Are there children who are alone?
- Are there children who are behaving in an aggressive and violent manner?
- Are children provided with culturally appropriate opportunities to talk about concerns, ideas and questions that they have?
- Do children have the opportunity to play?
- Are the special needs of unaccompanied children, long-stayers in camps and children in confinement being addressed?

Services

- Are education and other activities provided so that children are able to participate in regular development-enhancing activities and re-establish a sense of routine?
- Do refugee adults and children have access to social services to help address difficulties?
- Are systems in place to identify and assist children experiencing psychosocial distress?
- Are training and support being provided to teachers? Are primary healthcare and other service personnel available to help them better support children?
- Do specialised mental health services exist to which children in severe distress might be referred?

Source: UNICEF, adapted from *Refugee Children: Guidelines on Protection and Care*, UNHCR, 1994.

Appendix 2: School Feeding Programme Checklist

The following questions are important to ask if food is being considered as a resource for education interventions:

Programme Objectives
- If food is being proposed, how will it be used? School feeding, take-home rations, food for work, food for training, food for teachers?
- Why is a school feeding programme (or other) appropriate in the present situation?
- What are the objectives of this programme? Is the proposed use of food one that will help to meet identified needs in education? Will food attract significantly greater numbers of children to school?
- Which of these objectives are specific to the emergency situation?
- Do you have the necessary data to justify the need to address these objectives (nutrition status, enrolment and attendance statistics, etc.)?

Target Population
- Who are the target beneficiaries of the programme?
- Do you have the necessary data to determine those schools or regions most affected or most in need of assistance (food security status, literacy statistics, enrolment etc.)?
- Which groups might benefit from take-home rations (e.g. girls, minorities, etc.)?

Capacity Building, Sustainability and Coordination
- What capacity-building activities are necessary before the start of the programme?
- Do schools have proper infrastructure to support a school-feeding programme (e.g. access to water, cooking facilities, utensils, etc.)?
- What is the current demand for education among communities, parents, children themselves? How will food change this?
- How do communities, parents, teachers, students, education officials view the introduction of food? Does the use of food have the potential to create or aggravate tensions between and within communities?
- What infrastructure has to be in place before food delivery can begin? What procurement and contracting systems need to be arranged?
- What infrastructure has to be in place before food preparation and feeding to children can begin?
- What arrangements need to be made for the establishment of offices, warehouses and transport bases? Telecommunications? Vehicles and routes?
- Are there sufficient numbers of teachers and materials and is there adequate infrastructure to absorb and accommodate additional learners? What is the likelihood that the introduction of food may overwhelm an already overburdened education system?
- Will food be sustained? If so, how? What is the phase-out strategy for withdrawal of food aid? How will this have an impact on education?
- Are other humanitarian agencies working on education in the same or nearby areas? Do they plan to use food as a resource in their education programmes? If so, in what ways? Are they willing to coordinate? Will food be used evenly and consistently by different agencies? How might the uneven provision of food draw students and teachers from one school/area to another school/area?
- What are the staffing implications for us or our partners? Are current staff numbers

sufficient to take on the management of a food-assisted education programme without being diverted from current responsibilities? Is significant scale-up needed?

Selection of Commodities and Nutritional Considerations

- What food are you going to provide?
- Will the programme include take-home rations? How will the programme be monitored?
- What food commodities are available?
- Are there particular problems of disease, malnutrition or infestation among schoolchildren? If so, can specific micronutrient deficiencies be addressed through the selection of commodities or fortification?
- Culturally, what are the food preferences and tastes of the schoolchildren?

Addressing Food Safety, Health and Hygiene

- Are there sanitation facilities and potable water available at the schools?
- How can the programme design incorporate training in order to educate and empower food handlers?
- How can the risk of contamination be mitigated?
- Is there a problem of infestation with intestinal helminths amongst the schoolchildren? If so, will a provision for regular deworming treatments be a necessary part of the school feeding intervention?
- Are HIV/AIDS preventive education programmes currently available for schoolchildren?
- How can HIV/AIDS preventive education be incorporated into the design of the programme?
- What contingency plan will there be if teachers succumb to HIV/AIDS?

Timelines

- What is the likely duration of the assistance operation?
- What data are available for each phase of the operation (initial assessment, baseline study, monitoring and evaluation)?
- When will food be available?
- What capacity-building activities will there be prior to the start of the programme and what is the likely starting date?
- How will relief (and later recovery) assistance be phased out and how, where appropriate, will a smooth transition to a subsequent development phase be achieved?

Donors

- Who are the potential donors? When will donor resources be available?
- Has a comprehensive and detailed programme proposal about the ideal programme scenario been drafted for donors?
- How long will food be available from donors? Several months, 1-2 years, 5-10 years? *(If food is only available from donors for a period of several months, it might be better used for teacher incentives than for school feeding programmes, which may take at least that long to set up).*

Sources: Adapted from: World Food Programme, *Planning for School Feeding in the Emergency Setting – Situation Analysis, Designing the Programme, Implementation*, 2004, http://www.wfp.org; and Catholic Relief Services, *Checklist: Determining Whether to Use Food as a Resource*, www.crs.org.

3.   Teaching and Learning

Introduction

Deciding what is important to teach is difficult for all educators. In an emergency, important decisions will need to be made about the nature of education services offered, whether formal or non-formal; the curricula to be followed, whether from the country of origin or the host country; and priorities for learning, whether focused on survival, vocational skills or academic study. There may also be a need for curriculum revision or development.

It is vital that education is relevant for the learners. This requires working closely with and receiving direction from the community to determine their education needs. This normally means working through existing education systems, if possible, rather than setting up separate structures. It means emphasising the community's active participation in all education efforts, including decisions concerning learning content. The curricula adopted should be relevant to the present and anticipated future needs of the learners, and thus correlate with information that the community needs due to circumstances changed by the crisis, such as life skills, peace education, civic education, mine awareness, health, nutrition, HIV/AIDS, human rights and the environment. Supplementary life skills education should be available for children who are not in school, their parents, the elderly and marginalised groups.

Emergency education programmes are a form of psychosocial intervention as they establish a familiar learning environment, provide a regular schedule and instil a feeling of hope for the future. Everyone involved in providing education, especially teachers and school administrators, should receive an orientation in their role mitigating the psychological and social impact on the learners.

Education services should acknowledge that people learn in different ways and at different speeds and need to actively participate in the learning process. For people to learn effectively, participatory teaching and learning techniques, including learner-centred methodologies, are essential. Child-centred methods should address the needs of the whole person, teaching skills necessary for survival, individual development, social interaction and academic study. For adults, learning is life-long and experiential. Their learning will be enhanced when they can see the purpose, value and relevance of what they learn and they are given the opportunity to be active participants in their own learning.

When those teaching are untrained, it is crucial that they receive appropriate training, not only in basic subjects, but also in subjects especially relevant for emergency situations. Further training to cope with the psychosocial needs of the target population will also be needed.

Communities want to know that governments will recognise their children's education, and that their children will be able to use their education to gain access to higher education and employment. The main concern is whether governments, educational institutions and employers recognise the curricula and resulting certificates. Aside from legitimating student test performance, graduation certificates recognise students' achievements and motivate them to attend school. In refugee situations, certification typically involves substantial negotiations with both the asylum and home countries. Ideally, in longer-term refugee situations, the curricula need to 'face both ways' and be acceptable in both the country of origin and the host country. This requires significant regional and inter-agency coordination to harmonise educational activities and refugee caseloads in different countries.

Links to the standards common to all categories

The process by which an education response is developed and implemented is critical to its effectiveness. This section should be utilised in conjunction with the standards common to all categories, which cover community participation, local resources, initial assessment, response, monitoring and evaluation. In particular, the participation of disaster-affected people – including vulnerable groups – should be maximised to ensure its appropriateness and quality.

Minimum standards: these are qualitative in nature and specify the minimum levels to be attained in the provision of education response.

Key indicators: these are 'signals' that show whether the standard has been attained. They provide a way of measuring and communicating the impact, or result, of programmes as well as the process, or methods, used. The indicators may be qualitative or quantitative.

Guidance notes: these include specific points to consider when applying the standard and indicators in different situations, guidance on tackling practical difficulties, and advice on priority issues. They may also include critical issues relating to the standard or indicators, and describe dilemmas, controversies or gaps in current knowledge. Annex 2 includes a select list of references, which point to sources of information on both general issues and specific technical issues relating to this section.

Teaching and Learning

Standard 1 Curricula	Standard 2 Training	Standard 3 Instruction	Standard 4 Assessment
Culturally, socially and linguistically relevant curricula are used to provide formal and non-formal education, appropriate to the particular emergency situation.	Teachers and other education personnel receive periodic, relevant and structured training according to need and circumstances.	Instruction is learner-centred, participatory and inclusive.	Appropriate methods are used to evaluate and validate learning achievements.

Annex 2: References and Resource Guide
Teaching and Learning section

Teaching and learning standard 1: curricula

Culturally, socially and linguistically relevant curricula are used to provide formal and non-formal education, appropriate to the particular emergency situation.

Key indicators (to be read in conjunction with the guidance notes)

- Existing curricula are reviewed for appropriateness to the age or developmental level, language, culture, capacities and needs of the learners affected by the emergency. Curricula are used, adapted or enriched as necessary (see guidance notes 1-3).

- Where curriculum development or adaptation is required, it is conducted with the meaningful participation of stakeholders and considers the best interests and needs of the learners (see guidance notes 1-3).

- Curricula address life skills, literacy, numeracy and core competencies of basic education relevant to given stages of an emergency (see guidance notes 4-5).

- Curricula address the psychosocial well-being needs of teachers and learners in order for them to be better able to cope with life during and after the emergency (see guidance note 6).

- Learning content, materials and instruction are provided in the language(s) of the learners and the teachers, especially in the early years of learning (see guidance note 7).

- Curricula and methods of instruction respond to the current needs of learners and promote future learning opportunities (see guidance note 8).

- Curricula and instructional materials are gender-sensitive, recognise diversity and promote respect for learners (see guidance note 9).

- Sufficient teaching and learning materials are provided, as needed, in a timely manner to support relevant education activities. Preference is given to locally available materials for sustainability (see guidance note 10).

Guidance notes

1. *A curriculum may be defined* as a plan of action to help learners broaden their knowledge and skill base. For the purposes of the minimum standards, 'curriculum' is used as an umbrella term that applies to both formal and non-formal education programmes. It includes learning objectives, learning content, teaching methodologies and techniques, instructional materials and methods of assessment. Both formal and non-formal education programmes should be guided by a curriculum that builds on learners' knowledge and experience and is relevant to the immediate environment. For the minimum standards, the following definitions are used:
   - *learning objectives* identify the knowledge, skills, values and attitudes that will be developed through the education activities;
   - *learning content* is the material (knowledge, skills, values and attitudes) to be studied or learned;
   - *teaching methodology* refers to the approach chosen for, and used in, the presentation

of learning content;
- *teaching technique* or approach is a component of methodology and constitutes the process used to carry out the overall methodology; and
- *instructional material* refers to books, posters and other teaching and learning materials.

Relevant formal and non-formal education curricula should have quality learning content that is gender-sensitive, appropriate to the level of learning and is in the language(s) that both learners and teachers understand. Participatory methodologies should also be part of the curricula, to encourage learners to take a more active role in their learning (see Annex 1: Terminology on page 79 for definitions of 'quality education' and 'relevant education').

2. *Age-appropriate and developmental levels:* curricula should be examined to ensure that they are not only age-appropriate, but also that the developmental level is compatible with learners' progress. Age and developmental levels may vary widely within both non-formal and formal education programmes in emergencies, requiring an adaptation of curricula and methods. The term 'age-appropriate' refers to chronological age range, while 'developmentally appropriate' refers to the learners' actual needs and cognitive development.

3. *Curriculum development* can be a long and difficult process, but in emergencies curricula are often adapted from either the host country, the country of origin or other emergency settings. It is important to ensure that both formal and non-formal rapid start-up curricula consider the special needs of all learners, including children associated with fighting forces (CAFF), girls, learners over-aged for their grade level, school drop-outs and adult learners. It is equally important to ensure that stakeholders are actively involved in the design of curricula, as well as the periodic review of education programmes. A range of actors may be consulted, including learners, community members, teachers, facilitators, education authorities and programme managers, among others.

Where formal education programmes are being established during or after emergencies, preference should be given to using, and if necessary adapting and enriching, recognised primary and secondary school curricula. For formal education programmes for refugees, it is preferred to adopt the curricula of the country of origin to facilitate voluntary repatriation, although this is not always possible or appropriate. Refugee and host country perspectives should be fully considered in these decisions.

Ideally, in longer-term refugee situations, curricula need to 'face both ways' and be acceptable in both the country of origin and the host country. This requires substantial regional and inter-agency coordination to harmonise educational activities and refugee caseloads in different countries. Specific issues to be decided include language competencies and recognition of examination results for certification.

4. *Appropriate instructional methodologies* should be developed and tailored to suit the context, needs, age and capacities of learners. Implementation of new methodologies during the initial stages of an emergency may be stressful for experienced teachers, as well as learners, parents and community members, who could perceive this as too much change and too fast. Education in emergencies or in early reconstruction should offer teachers in a formal education setting an opportunity for change, but transition to more participatory or learner-friendly methods of instruction must be introduced with care and

sensitivity. With non-formal education interventions, learner-centred approaches may be introduced more quickly through the training of volunteers, animators and facilitators.

5. *Core competencies* should be identified prior to the development or adaptation of learning content or teacher training materials. Beyond functional literacy and numeracy, 'core competencies of basic education' refers to the essential knowledge, skills, attitudes and practice required by learners in an emergency-affected population to participate actively and meaningfully as members of their community or country.

6. *The psychosocial needs and development* of learners, as well as education personnel, must be considered and addressed at all stages of an emergency, including crisis and recovery. All education personnel, formal and non-formal, should be trained in recognising signs of distress in learners and steps to take to address and respond to this behaviour in the learning environment. Referral mechanisms should be clearly outlined for education personnel to provide additional support to learners who exhibit severe distress. Teaching methods for child and youth populations who have been exposed to trauma should include predictable structure, shorter learning periods to build concentration, positive disciplinary methods, involvement of all students in learning activities, and cooperative games.

The psychosocial needs of education personnel will also need to be considered, as personnel are often drawn from the affected population and face the same stressors or trauma as learners. Training, monitoring and follow-up support should clearly consider these factors (see Access and Learning Environment Appendix 1 on page 49 for a Psychosocial Checklist; see also Access and learning environment standard 2 on page 45 and Teachers and other education personnel standard 3 on page 69).

7. *Language:* it is not uncommon for asylum countries to insist that refugee education programmes comply with their standards, including the use of their own language(s) and curricula. However, it is important to consider the future of the learners, especially those who wish to continue their studies after the emergency. Humanitarian actors should strongly encourage host governments to permit refugees to study in their home or national language(s). If this is allowed, all significant learning content, teacher guides, student texts and other written and audio-visual materials not in the home language of the learners and teachers will need to be translated into the language of instruction. If this is not allowed, supplementary classes and activities in the language of the learners should be developed.

8. *Learning content and key concepts:* when determining learning content, consideration should be given to the knowledge, skills and language(s) useful for learners at each stage of an emergency and those skills that would enhance their capacity to lead independent, productive lives both during and after the emergency and to be able to continue to access learning opportunities.

Appropriate learning content and key concepts should draw on the following:
  – skills-based health education (appropriate to age and situation): first aid, reproductive health, sexually transmitted infections, HIV/AIDS;
  – human rights and humanitarian norms; active citizenship; peace education/peace building; non-violence; conflict prevention/management/resolution; child protection; security and safety;

– cultural activities, such as music, dance, drama, sports and games;
– information necessary for survival in the new environment: landmine and unexploded ordnance awareness, rapid evacuation, and access to services;
– child development and adolescence; and
– livelihood skills and vocational training.

9. *Diversity* should be considered in the design and implementation of educational activities at all stages of an emergency, in particular the inclusion of diverse learners, inclusion of teachers/facilitators from diverse backgrounds and promotion of tolerance and respect. Aspects to consider in encouraging diversity may include, among others, gender, culture, nationality, ethnicity, religion, learning capacity, learners with special education needs, and multi-level and multi-age instruction.

10. *Locally available materials* for learners should be assessed at the onset of an emergency. For refugees, this includes materials from their country or area of origin. Materials should be adapted, developed or procured and made available in sufficient quantities. Monitoring of storage, distribution and usage of all materials is required. Learners should be able to relate to the learning content and materials should reflect and be respectful of the culture of the learners.

Teaching and learning standard 2: training

Teachers and other education personnel receive periodic, relevant and structured training according to need and circumstances.

Key indicators (to be read in conjunction with the guidance notes)

- Training corresponds to prioritised needs, objectives of education activities and learning content (see guidance note 1-2).

- Where appropriate, training is recognised and approved by relevant education authorities (see guidance notes 3-4).

- Qualified trainers conduct the training courses and provision is made for ongoing support and guidance, appropriate follow-up, monitoring and supervision in the field, and refresher training (see guidance note 4).

- Training, including follow-up monitoring, encourages the teacher to be a facilitator in the learning environment, promotes participatory methods of teaching, and demonstrates the use of teaching aids.

- Training content is regularly assessed to determine if it meets the needs of teachers, students and the community, and is revised when necessary.

- Training provides teachers with appropriate skills to be able to assume leadership roles when required by members of the community.

Guidance notes

1. *'Teacher'* refers to both instructors in formal education programmes and facilitators or animators in non-formal education programmes (see Teachers and other education personnel standards 1-3 on pages 65-69 for information on recruitment and selection, conditions of work and support and supervision).

2. *The development of training curricula and content* should be based on the particular needs of education personnel in the context of the situation, within budget and time constraints. Training programmes should address the challenges of value-based education during times of emergency and should incorporate life skills and peace education, as needed.

   Training curricula may include, but are not limited to: core subject knowledge; pedagogy and teaching methodologies; child development; teaching adults; respect for diversity; teaching of learners with special needs; psychosocial needs and development; conflict prevention/resolution and peace education; human rights and children's rights; codes of conduct; life skills for teachers (including HIV/AIDS); school-community relations; utilising community resources; and identifying and meeting needs of transient or returning populations, such as internally displaced populations or refugees.

3. *Training support and coordination:* once the emergency has stabilised, national and local education authorities and community education committees should be involved in the design and implementation of formal and non-formal teacher training activities, whenever possible. It is advisable to start a dialogue on curricula for in-service teacher training, and mechanisms for recognition of training received, at the beginning of the emergency response. However, in many refugee situations there is often no connection between the refugee community and its education programmes and the local education system.

   Where possible, local trainers should be identified to develop and implement appropriate training for teachers, with capacity building for their facilitation and training skills as needed. Where there are limited numbers of trainers available or they are themselves inadequately trained, external agencies (e.g. United Nations, international NGOs) and local, national and regional institutions should make coordinated efforts to strengthen existing or transitional structures and institutions providing in-service and pre-service teacher training.

4. *Recognition and accreditation:* approval and accreditation by national and local education authorities is sought in part to ensure quality and recognition in the immediate situation and in part with a view to the post-emergency situation. In the case of refugee teachers, the education authorities of the host or home country/area, or at least one of these, should recognise the training. For this purpose, it is essential that teacher training courses are well structured and well documented, and meet the teacher qualification requirements of the education authorities, as well as including any additional components related to the emergency.

Teaching and learning standard 3: instruction

Instruction is learner-centred, participatory and inclusive.

Key indicators (to be read in conjunction with the guidance notes)

- Learners are provided with opportunities to be actively engaged in their own learning (see guidance note 1).

- Participatory methods are used to facilitate learner involvement in their own learning and to improve the learning environment.

- Through practice and interaction with learners, teachers demonstrate an understanding of lesson content and of the teaching skills acquired during training courses.

- Instruction addresses the needs of all learners, including those with special needs, by promoting inclusiveness and reducing barriers to learning (see guidance note 2).

- Parents and community leaders understand and accept the learning content and teaching methods used (see guidance note 3).

Guidance notes

1. *Active engagement:* teaching should be interactive and participatory. It should also make use of developmentally appropriate teaching and learning methods. This may involve, among other methods: group work, project work, peer education, role-play, narratives, games, videos and stories. Active learning helps to build reciprocal relationships between the teacher and the learners, and between learners, and also helps to ensure positive psychosocial well-being (see Access and learning environment standard 2, guidance note 6 on page 46).

2. *Learning barriers:* teachers should be trained to talk with parents, community members, education leaders and other stakeholders about the importance of formal and non-formal education activities in emergency settings, as well as to discuss issues of diversity, inclusion and outreach. Dialogue with education leaders, parents and community members is needed to ensure their understanding of and support for inclusion, as well as the provision of appropriate resource materials.

3. *Choice and use of methods of instruction* will require consideration of the education, experience, training and needs of the teachers. Teachers will need to be familiar with changed content as well as with changes expected in teacher awareness and behaviour. The involvement and acceptance of parents, the community and traditional and religious leaders is instrumental in fine-tuning activities and methods of instruction to meet community concerns.

Teaching and learning standard 4: assessment

Appropriate methods are used to evaluate and validate learning achievements.

Key indicators (to be read in conjunction with the guidance notes)

- Differentiated continuous assessment and evaluation methods are in place to assess learning periodically and appropriately. Procedures are in place to use this information to improve the quality of instruction (see guidance note 1).

- Learner achievement is recognised and credits or course completion documents are provided accordingly (see guidance note 2).

- Assessment and evaluation methods are considered fair, reliable and non-threatening to the learner (see guidance note 3).

Guidance notes

1. *Effective assessment and evaluation methods and measures* should be put in place that reflect consideration of:
   - *relevance* (e.g. tests and examinations are relevant and appropriate to the learning context);
   - *consistency* (e.g. evaluation methods are known and applied in a similar way at all locations or by all teachers);
   - *opportunity* (absent learners are offered another assessment opportunity);
   - *timing* (assessment occurs during and at the end of instruction);
   - *frequency* (which may be affected by the emergency);
   - *appropriate setting* (an appropriate setting or facility is available during formal assessments, conducted by appropriate education personnel); and
   - *stakeholders and transparency* (assessment results are shared with learners and, with respect to children, their parents).

2. *Assessment results:* in the case of formal education programmes, assessment should be conducted in such a way that learners' achievements and examination results can be recognised by the education authorities of the host country and/or home country. In the case of refugees, efforts should be made to obtain recognition by the education authorities of the country or area of origin. Course completion documents may include, but not be limited to, diplomas, graduation certificates, etc.

3. *Assessment code of ethics:* assessment and evaluation should be developed and implemented according to a code of ethics. Assessments and evaluations should be considered fair and reliable and should be conducted in a way that does not increase fear and trauma. Care should be taken that there is no harassment of learners in return for good marks or promotions within a school or programme.

4.   Teachers and Other Education Personnel

Introduction

All aspects of humanitarian assistance rely on the skills, knowledge and commitment of staff and volunteers working in difficult and sometimes insecure conditions. The demands placed upon them can be considerable, and if they are to meet minimum standards, it is essential that they are suitably trained, managed and monitored, and provided with the necessary materials, support and supervision.

In emergency settings, the recruitment and selection of teachers and education personnel must be participatory and transparent and based on set criteria. When possible, education staff should be drawn from the affected population. This allows for integration into education programmes of cultural traditions, customs and experiences that respect the positive practices, belief systems and needs of the affected population(s).

Once recruited, teachers and education personnel should work together with the community to develop a code of conduct and defined conditions of work. Teachers and other education personnel must be employed under clear contractual arrangements, which spell out their entitlements (salary or incentive, working days and hours, working conditions, etc.) and their responsibilities and duties. The code of conduct should set out clear standards of behaviour for teachers and education personnel and specify the consequences for persons who do not comply with these standards. Obtaining the support of the affected population for education will help both the process of recruiting and keeping teachers and education personnel and the willingness of parents to send their children to school.

In areas of crisis, teachers and education personnel, like everyone else in the community, have to come to terms with what they have experienced and try to rebuild their lives. Both formal and non-formal education programme staff need support to cope with the emergency and to help deal with the trauma and stress resulting from the disaster or conflict. Support mechanisms should be provided that help them support each other, as well as equip them with the tools and skills necessary to improve the well-being of learners.

Appropriate training of teachers and other education personnel is essential for the success of education in emergency programmes. Standards for training are found in the section on Teaching and Learning.

Teachers and education personnel also need support in the form of supervision. At the community level, parents, village leaders, community education committees and local government officials need training in how to monitor and support the education programmes in their areas. When affected populations are empowered to take control of their education programmes, they exercise their right to self-reliance and can find solutions to their problems. Community participation in the support and supervision of education personnel promotes a productive relationship between the community and the teacher in the learning environment.

The performance of school management, teachers and other education personnel should be constantly monitored and evaluated to ensure quality and the continued support of the affected population. It is important that the monitoring and evaluation take the form of guidance, not only of control. Monitoring and participatory evaluation are integral to improving teacher performance and practice. Staff performance appraisals, as much as possible, should be a positive learning experience for teachers.

Links to the standards common to all categories

The process by which an education response is developed and implemented is critical to its effectiveness. This section should be utilised in conjunction with the standards common to all categories, which cover community participation, local resources, initial assessment, response, monitoring and evaluation. In particular, the participation of disaster-affected people – including vulnerable groups – should be maximised to ensure its appropriateness and quality.

Minimum standards: these are qualitative in nature and specify the minimum levels to be attained in the provision of education response.

Key indicators: these are 'signals' that show whether the standard has been attained. They provide a way of measuring and communicating the impact, or result, of programmes as well as the process, or methods, used. The indicators may be qualitative or quantitative.

Guidance notes: these include specific points to consider when applying the standard and indicators in different situations, guidance on tackling practical difficulties, and advice on priority issues. They may also include critical issues relating to the standard or indicators, and describe dilemmas, controversies or gaps in current knowledge. Annex 2 includes a select list of references, which point to sources of information on both general issues and specific technical issues relating to this section.

Teachers and Other Education Personnel

Standard 1
Recruitment and selection

A sufficient number of appropriately qualified teachers and other education personnel is recruited through a participatory and transparent process based on selection criteria that reflect diversity and equity.

Standard 2
Conditions of work

Teachers and other education personnel have clearly defined conditions of work, follow a code of conduct and are appropriately compensated.

Standard 3
Support and supervision

Supervision and support mechanisms are established for teachers and other education personnel, and are used on a regular basis.

Appendix 1
Code of Conduct

Annex 2: References and Resource Guide
Teachers and Other Education Personnel section

Teachers and other education personnel standard 1: recruitment and selection

A sufficient number of appropriately qualified teachers and other education personnel is recruited through a participatory and transparent process based on selection criteria that reflect diversity and equity.

Key indicators (to be read in conjunction with the guidance notes)

- Clear and appropriate job descriptions are developed prior to the recruitment process (see guidance note 1).

- Clear guidelines exist for the recruitment process.

- A selection committee, including community representatives, selects teachers based on a transparent assessment of candidates' competencies and considerations of gender, diversity and acceptance by the community (see guidance notes 2-5).

- The number of teachers recruited and deployed is sufficient to prevent over-sized classes (see guidance note 6).

Guidance notes

1. *Job descriptions* should include, among other components, roles and responsibilities and clear reporting lines, as well as a code of conduct.

2. *Experience and qualifications:* in an emergency, the aim should be to recruit qualified teachers with recognised qualifications but, in some situations, those with little or no experience will need to be considered. Training will therefore be required in these cases. If qualified teachers no longer have certificates or other documents, it is important to provide alternative means of verification, such as testing of applicants. While the minimum age for teachers should be 18, it may be necessary to appoint younger teachers. In some situations, it is necessary to proactively recruit female teachers and to adjust the recruitment criteria or process to promote gender parity, where possible and appropriate.

   It is necessary to recruit teachers who speak the home language(s) of learners from minorities who are taught in a national language not their own. Where possible and appropriate, intensive courses in the national and/or host country language(s) should be provided (see also Teaching and learning standard 1, guidance note 7 on page 58).

3. *Criteria may include the following:*
   - professional qualifications: academic, teaching or psychosocial experience; other skills/experience; relevant language ability;
   - personal qualifications: age; gender (recruiters should aim for gender balance if possible); ethnic and religious background; diversity (to ensure representation of the community);

– other qualifications: acceptance by and interaction with the community; belonging to the affected population.

4. *Selection:* teachers and other education personnel should primarily be selected from among the affected population, but if necessary can be recruited from outside. If a site is established for refugees or internally displaced populations, applications from eligible local candidates may be accepted if this will help to foster good relations. Selection should be carried out in consultation with the community, the host community and local authorities.

5. *References:* in crisis settings, a reference check should be carried out for teachers and education personnel to avoid employing individuals who could have an adverse effect on learners and/or who do not fully respect their rights.

6. *A locally realistic standard* should be set for maximum class size, and every effort made to recruit enough teachers to avoid major deviations from this standard. Monitoring reports should indicate the number of over-sized classes at the different levels of schooling.

Teachers and other education personnel standard 2: conditions of work

Teachers and other education personnel have clearly defined conditions of work, follow a code of conduct and are appropriately compensated.

Key indicators (to be read in conjunction with the guidance notes)

- Compensation and conditions of work are specified in a job contract, and compensation is provided on a regular basis, related to the level of professionalism and efficiency of work (see guidance notes 1-2).

- International actors coordinate with education authorities, community education committees and NGOs to develop appropriate strategies, and agree to use fair, acceptable and sustainable remuneration scales for the various categories and levels of teachers and other education personnel (see guidance note 2).

- The code of conduct and defined conditions of work are developed in a participatory manner, involving both education personnel and community members, and there are clear implementation guidelines (see guidance notes 1 and 3).

- The code of conduct is signed and followed by education personnel, and appropriate measures are documented and applied in cases of misconduct and/or violation of the code of conduct (see guidance notes 3-4).

Guidance notes

1. *Conditions of work* should specify job description, compensation, attendance, hours/days of work, length of contract, support and supervision mechanisms, and dispute resolution mechanisms (see also standard 1, guidance note 1 above).

2. *Compensation* can be monetary or non-monetary, should be appropriate (as agreed upon), and paid regularly. The appropriate level of compensation should be determined through a participatory process ensuring coordination between the actors involved. It should aim to be at a level that ensures professionalism and continuity of service and sustainability. In particular, it should be sufficient to enable teachers to focus on their professional work rather than having to seek additional sources of income to meet their basic needs. Compensation should be contingent on adherence to the conditions of work and code of conduct.

Care should be taken to avoid a situation where teachers from different backgrounds (e.g. nationals and refugees) receive different levels of pay. Key actors should be involved in the development of long-term strategies for a sustainable compensation system. There should be coordination between United Nations agencies, NGOs, education authorities and other organisations to determine common levels of compensation.

3. *The code of conduct* should set clear standards of behaviour for education personnel and specify the mandatory consequences for persons who do not comply with these standards. The code should apply to the learning environment and to education programme events or activities (see Appendix 1 on page 70 for a sample code of conduct).

The code should ensure that teachers and education personnel promote a positive learning environment and the well-being of learners. The code should state, among other things, that education personnel:
   − exhibit professional behaviour by maintaining a high standard of conduct, self-control and moral/ethical behaviour;
   − participate in creating an environment in which all students are accepted;
   − maintain a safe and healthy environment, free from harassment (including sexual harassment), intimidation, abuse and violence, and discrimination;
   − maintain regular attendance and punctuality;
   − demonstrate professionalism and efficiency in their work; and
   − exhibit other behaviours as deemed appropriate by the community and education stakeholders.

4. *Code implementation guidelines:* there should be training on the code of conduct for all education and non-education personnel who work in the learning environment. Training and support should be provided to members of community education committees and education supervisors and managers on their roles and responsibilities in monitoring the implementation of codes of conduct. They should also be helped to identify and incorporate key concerns around codes of conduct into school/non-formal education programme action plans. Supervisory mechanisms should establish transparent reporting and monitoring procedures, which protect the confidentiality of all parties involved (see also standard 3 below).

Teachers and other education personnel standard 3: support and supervision

Supervision and support mechanisms are established for teachers and other education personnel, and are used on a regular basis.

Key indicators (to be read in conjunction with the guidance notes)

- A supervisory mechanism provides for regular assessment, monitoring and support for teachers and other education personnel (see guidance notes 1-2).

- Staff performance appraisals are conducted, written up and discussed with the individual(s) concerned on a regular basis (see guidance note 3).

- Appropriate and accessible psychosocial support and counselling are provided to teachers and other education personnel, as needed (see guidance note 4).

Guidance notes

1. *Supervisory mechanisms:* each country or affected area should define standards for teachers and education personnel and develop and implement a support and supervision mechanism. This mechanism may include representatives from the community (including traditional and religious leaders), community school organisations such as parent-teacher associations, local authorities, head teachers and teachers' unions. The supervisory mechanism should be closely linked to the community education committee. The committee should include in its terms of reference the monitoring of education personnel in relation to codes of conduct, with a focus on professionalism, work efficiency and appropriate conduct (see also Community participation standard 1 on page 15).

2. *Training:* see Teaching and learning standard 2 on page 59 for information on education staff training.

3. *Staff performance appraisals* should include an assessment of the efficiency and effectiveness of the teachers or other education personnel and should provide consultation opportunities for teachers, head teachers and other relevant personnel to identify issues and develop follow-up activities that are agreed upon collaboratively. Where appropriate, appraisals should recognise and celebrate achievement in order to motivate education personnel. Monitoring and participatory evaluation may motivate teachers and increase their competence.

4. *Crisis support:* even trained and experienced teachers and other education personnel may find themselves traumatised by events and faced with new challenges and responsibilities vis-à-vis learners, and their ability to cope and perform depends on relevant support being available. A support mechanism should be established in the community to assist teachers and other education personnel dealing with crisis situations.

Teaching and Learning: Appendix

Appendix 1: Teacher's Code of Conduct

At all times, the teacher:
- acts in a manner that maintains the honour and dignity of the profession
- protects the confidentiality of anything said by a student in confidence
- protects students from conditions which interfere with learning or are harmful to the students' health and safety
- does not take advantage of his or her position to profit in any way
- does not sexually harass any student or have any manner of sexual relationship with a student
- is a good, honest role model.

In the classroom, the teacher:
- promotes a positive and safe learning environment
- teaches in a manner that respects the dignity and rights of all students
- promotes students' self-esteem, confidence and self-worth
- promotes high expectations of students and helps each student to reach his/her potential
- encourages students to develop as active, responsible and effective learners
- creates an atmosphere of trust.

In their professional life, the teacher:
- displays a basic competence in educational methodology and his/her subject
- displays an understanding (in his/her teaching) of how children learn
- is always on time for class and prepared to teach
- does not engage in activities that adversely affect the quality of his/her teaching
- takes advantage of all professional development opportunities and uses modern, accepted teaching methods
- teaches principles of good citizenship, peace and social responsibility
- honestly represents each student's performance and examination results.

With respect to the community, the teacher:
- encourages parents to support and participate in their children's learning
- recognises the importance of family and community involvement in school
- supports and promotes a positive image of the school.

In addition to the items mentioned here, the teacher is expected to abide by all other rules and policies of the wider environment (camp, school, etc).

Source: This code of conduct was used by UNHCR Eritrea as a model, which schools then adapted for themselves.

5.   Education Policy and Coordination

Introduction

International instruments and declarations proclaim the right of all individuals to have an education, which sets the foundation for the promotion of all human rights. The right to free expression, the right to equality and the right to have a voice in decision-making with regard to social and educational policies are integral parts of education.

In emergency settings it is essential that these rights are preserved. As part of the emergency response, education authorities and key stakeholders should develop and implement an education plan that takes into account national and international educational policies, upholds the right to education, and is responsive to the learning needs of affected populations. This framework should aim to improve the quality of education and access to schools and should clearly show the transition from emergency response to development. Community involvement in the planning and implementation of interventions, programmes and policies is vital to the success of any emergency response.

In emergency situations, there is often a lack of coordination, with education programmes being conducted independently by different stakeholders. Inter-agency coordination mechanisms are needed at settlement/community, district, national and regional level, and they must be inclusive and transparent. Such mechanisms are essential for conducting needs assessments, developing standardised approaches, and sharing resources and information between all actors and stakeholders.

Education should be coordinated within the larger initial humanitarian response of food, shelter, health, and water and sanitation interventions. Education responses, based upon known good practices, should be tailored to the needs of the community within the specific context of the emergency. Survival skills such as landmine, hygiene and HIV/AIDS awareness campaigns should be provided to all age groups.

Links to the standards common to all categories

The process by which an education response is developed and implemented is critical to its effectiveness. This section should be utilised in conjunction with the standards common to all categories, which cover community participation, local resources, initial assessment, response, monitoring and evaluation. In particular, the participation of disaster-affected people – including vulnerable groups – should be maximised to ensure its appropriateness and quality.

Minimum standards: these are qualitative in nature and specify the minimum levels to be attained in the provision of education response.

Key indicators: these are 'signals' that show whether the standard has been attained. They provide a way of measuring and communicating the impact, or result, of programmes as well as the process, or methods, used. The indicators may be qualitative or quantitative.

Guidance notes: these include specific points to consider when applying the standard and indicators in different situations, guidance on tackling practical difficulties, and advice on priority issues. They may also include critical issues relating to the standard or indicators, and describe dilemmas, controversies or gaps in current knowledge. Annex 2 includes a select list of references, which point to sources of information on both general issues and specific technical issues relating to this section.

Education Policy and Coordination

Standard 1
Policy formulation and enactment

Education authorities prioritise free access to schooling for all, and enact flexible policies to promote inclusion and education quality, given the emergency context.

Standard 2
Planning and implementation

Emergency education activities take into account national and international educational policies and standards and the learning needs of affected populations.

Standard 3
Coordination

There is a transparent coordination mechanism for emergency education activities, including effective information sharing between stakeholders.

Annex 2: References and Resource Guide
Education Policy and Coordination section

Education policy and coordination standard 1: policy formulation and enactment

Education authorities prioritise free access to schooling for all, and enact flexible policies to promote inclusion and education quality, given the education context.

Key indicators (to be read in conjunction with the guidance notes)

- Both during and after emergencies, education laws and policies uphold the right to education articulated in international human rights instruments and declarations (see guidance notes 1-2).

- Laws, regulations and policies protect against discrimination in education with regard to vulnerable and marginalised groups (see guidance note 3).

- Laws, regulations and policies are in place to ensure learners are not denied education because of limited resources of the learner or the learner's family (see guidance note 4).

- Laws, regulations and policies do not prevent schools for refugees from using curricula from the country or area of origin.

- Laws, regulations and policies permit the establishment of emergency education facilities by non-government actors when needed, subject to the education authority's guidance and inspection.

- Laws, regulations and policies are disseminated in a form that can be understood by all stakeholders.

- Policy promotes the development and use of an Education Management Information System (EMIS) database, to be used as a tool for analysing and reacting to changes in educational access and completion (see guidance note 5).

- National education policies are supported with legal and budgetary frameworks that permit a quick response to emergency situations (see guidance note 6).

Guidance notes

1. *International human rights instruments and declarations* that should be upheld include, but are not limited to, the United Nations Convention on the Rights of the Child (1989), the Universal Declaration of Human Rights (1948), the International Covenant on Economic, Social and Cultural Rights (1966), the Convention on the Elimination of All Forms of Discrimination Against Women (1979), and the Dakar Framework for Action: Education for All (2000).

Instruments and legal frameworks also include international rules with regard to the care of populations, with an emphasis on children and youth in areas such as mental health, nutrition, recreation, culture, prevention of abuse and initial education for children under six years, among others (see also Access and learning environment standard 1, guidance note 2 on page 43).

2. *Refugees, displaced and host populations:* all relevant stakeholders should collaborate to advocate that education reaches all groups in an equitable manner. This includes upholding the 1951 Convention Relating to the Status of Refugees, Article 22 (Public Education), which declares that refugees have the same education entitlements as nationals at the elementary level, and at higher levels should have access to studies, recognition of certificates, diplomas, degrees, remission of fees/charges and access to scholarships, on terms not less favourable than those applicable to aliens. While not afforded special protection, internally displaced populations should be afforded similar entitlements. Agencies should likewise advocate for the educational rights of national students, in refugee-receiving countries or areas and in countries affected by war.

3. *Marginalised groups* are population groups within a society or community whose interests are not represented by the core polity of the society. Marginalised groups are identified according to socio-economic or cultural characteristics, such as a person's income or wealth, ethnicity or race, gender, geographical location, religion, citizenship status, internal displacement or physical or mental condition. Asylum-seeker children should enjoy the right to education, since the Convention on the Rights of the Child applies to all children and adolescents under the age of 18 present within the territory of the state (see also Access and learning environment standard 1, guidance note 1 on page 42).

4. *Costs of education:* no learner should be denied access to education programmes due to inability to meet the costs of attendance, either in terms of fees or other associated costs, such as learning materials or uniforms. Every effort should be made to reduce the indirect costs of schooling, such as transportation and lost income, so that all children, youth and adults are able to participate.

5. *EMIS data* should be linked to information on areas and population groups that are prone to particular kinds of emergencies. This is a preparedness strategy that should provide input into national and local education planning. Where possible, educational data should be collected by the community and fed into a national EMIS system. Supporting organisations should help communities to identify means by which student enrolment, retention and completion can be increased, and also to address the needs of non-school going youth (see also Analysis standards 1 on page 21 and 3 on page 25).

6. *Emergency frameworks:* education should be included in the national disaster preparedness framework and resources should be secured to provide an effective and timely education response. International actors supporting national or local education development programmes should promote preparedness for emergency education response as a component of these programmes.

Education policy and coordination standard 2: planning and implementation

Emergency education activities take into account international and national educational policies and standards and the learning needs of affected populations.

Key indicators (to be read in conjunction with the guidance notes)

- International and national legal frameworks and policies are reflected in the education programmes of relief and development agencies (see guidance note 1).

- Emergency education programmes are planned and implemented in a manner that provides for their integration into longer-term development of the education sector.

- Education authorities and other key actors develop national and local education plans for current and future emergencies, and create a system for their regular revision (see guidance note 2).

- During and after emergencies, all stakeholders work together to implement a plan for education response that is linked to the most recent needs assessment and builds upon the previous education experience, policies and practices of the affected population(s).

- Education responses specify the financial, technical and human resources needed for effective planning, implementation and monitoring. Stakeholders ensure that the resources needed are made available (see guidance note 3).

- Planning and implementation of educational activities are integrated with other emergency response sectors (see guidance note 4).

Guidance notes

1. *Meeting education rights and goals:* education programmes should provide inclusive educational activities in line with international frameworks, such as the Convention on the Rights of the Child (1989), the Universal Declaration of Human Rights (1948), Education for All framework (2000) and the Millennium Development Goals (2000), in addition to applicable frameworks and policies of the relevant education authorities.

2. *National education plans* should indicate the actions to be taken in current or future emergencies with regard to programmes, actors, stakeholders, decision-making and coordination, as well as security and protection factors and mechanisms for inter-sectoral coordination. The plan should be supported by the appropriate education policy and frameworks. Contingency plans should be prepared for the education sector in relation to possible natural disasters (e.g. flooding, earthquake, hurricane) and, where relevant, for potential refugee or returnee influxes that may affect a local or national education system (see also Community participation standard 1, guidance note 5 on page 16 and standard 3 below).

3. *Resources:* authorities, donors, NGOs and other stakeholders should work together to ensure that adequate funding is secured for emergency education programmes that focus on learning, recreation and related activities designed to meet psychosocial needs. As emergencies stabilise, opportunities for education programming may be expanded to include early childhood development, formal primary and secondary schooling and adult literacy and vocational programmes, among others. Resource allocation should be balanced to augment physical elements (such as additional classrooms, textbooks and teaching and learning materials) and qualitative components (such as teacher and supervisory training courses).

4. *Sphere Minimum Standards:* special effort should be made to link the education action plan and its implementation to the Sphere minimum standards in the areas of:
   – water, sanitation and hygiene promotion;
   – food security, nutrition and food aid;
   – shelter, settlement and non-food items; and
   – health services (see the Linkages to Sphere Standards annex on the MSEE CD-ROM for Sphere-related standards).

Education policy and coordination standard 3: coordination

There is a transparent coordination mechanism for emergency education activities, including effective information sharing between stakeholders.

Key indicators (to be read in conjunction with the guidance notes)

● Education authorities establish an inter-agency coordination committee for current and future emergency response, which assumes the major role in planning and coordinating emergency education activities (see guidance note 1).

● When the education authority is not present or is unable to lead coordination, an inter-agency coordination committee provides guidance and coordination of education activities and programmes (see guidance note 1).

● Authorities, donors and other agencies establish financing structures that are coordinated with and support activities of education stakeholders (see guidance note 2).

● A common statement of coordination aims, indicators and monitoring procedures is in place, and all education actors commit themselves to work within that framework and make key information and statistics available in the public domain (see guidance note 3).

● Affected communities are authorised and able to participate in decision-making that directly affects them, particularly in policy or programme formulation, implementation and monitoring.

● A transparent and active mechanism exists for sharing information across sectors and between key national and international stakeholders (see guidance note 4).

Guidance notes

1. *Inter-agency coordination committee:* representatives should include a wide spectrum of stakeholders, wherever possible under the leadership of the education authority. Coordination committees may be needed at regional, national, district or local levels, depending on the nature of the emergency. Where education authorities lack capacity or legitimacy, leadership may be assigned by agreement to different agencies, but a representative of the local authority should always be a member of the committee. As soon as conditions permit, responsibility for coordination should be transferred to the appropriate authorities.

2. *Financing:* sufficient funds are required for successful and timely implementation of education programmes in emergencies. Every effort should be made to ensure transparent and coordinated approaches to financing, especially where salary payment systems for teacher compensation are inadequate or non-functional. Emergency financing arrangements should take into consideration local labour market conditions and traditions and should avoid setting precedents that cannot be sustained.

3. *Key coordination challenges* should be identified and addressed from an early stage in the emergency phase, in order to achieve a cost-effective approach that leads to sustainable and harmonised future education services. Issues may include teacher training, certification and payment; curriculum and related components (textbooks and teaching and learning aids); and structuring and recognition of schooling and examinations.

4. *Joint policy development and training workshops* should be developed collaboratively with education authorities and external actors to ensure good communications, promote collaboration and commitment to a shared vision, and enhance the overall development of the education system.

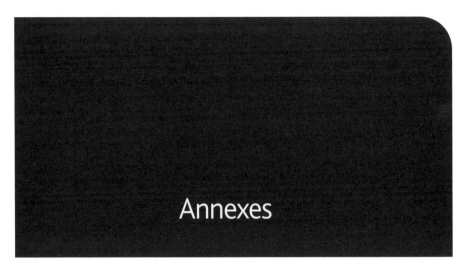

Annexes

Annex 1: Terminology

- **Access:** Access is the unrestricted opportunity to enrol in, attend and complete a formal or non-formal education programme. 'Unrestricted opportunity' means there are no practical, financial, physical, security-related, structural, institutional or socio-cultural obstacles impeding children, youth and adults from participating in and/or completing an education programme.

- **Basic education:** A basic education is the foundation for lifelong learning and human development, and encompasses both formal and non-formal programmes. Every person – child, youth and adult – should be able to benefit from educational opportunities designed to meet their basic learning needs. These needs comprise both the essential learning tools (such as literacy, oral expression, numeracy and problem-solving) and the basic learning content (such as knowledge, skills, values and attitudes) required by human beings to be able to survive, develop their full capacities to live, make informed decisions and continue learning. The scope of basic learning needs and how they should be met varies with individual countries and cultures, and inevitably changes with the passage of time.[1]

- **Children associated with fighting forces (CAFF):** During emergencies and crises, children are often associated with fighting forces – both state and non-state – either through abduction, recruitment, forced conscription or 'voluntary' action. These children do not always take up arms, but may also be porters, spies, cooks or gravely abused sexual victims. All of these children share the experience of being in a fighting force and being deprived of the opportunity for education. During demobilisation and reintegration processes, special attention must be given to the specific educational needs of such children, including formal and non-formal education, accelerated learning, life skills and vocational learning. Particular attention needs to be given to girls, who are consistently overlooked and omitted from rehabilitation programmes.

[1] World Education Forum, (26-28 April 2000). The Dakar Framework for Action: Education for All (by 2015).

- **Community education committee:** A committee established to identify and address the educational needs of a community, with representatives from parents and/or parent-teacher associations, local agencies, civil society associations, community organisations and youth and women's groups, among others, as well as teachers and learners (where appropriate). It may have sub-committees whose members are represented in its composition. In some cases, community education committees will be responsible for a single education programme, in others for several education programmes in a particular location.

- **Community participation:** 'Community participation' refers to both the processes and activities that allow members of an affected population to be heard, empowering them to be part of decision-making processes and enabling them to take direct action on education issues. Active involvement of the community facilitates the identification of community-specific education issues and strategies that are effective in addressing them. Additionally, community participation serves as a strategy to identify and mobilise local resources within a community, as well as build consensus and support for education programmes. Community participation must include real and sustained empowerment and capacity building, and must build upon efforts already under way on the ground.

- **Complex emergency:** A situation where the lives, well-being and dignity of the populations concerned are endangered by various crisis factors, such as natural and man-made disasters, civil unrest and armed conflict.

- **Curriculum:** A plan of action to help learners broaden their knowledge and skills base. For the purposes of the minimum standards, 'curriculum' is used as an umbrella term that applies to formal and non-formal education programmes. It includes learning objectives, learning content, teaching methodologies and techniques, instructional materials and methods of assessment. Both formal and non-formal education programmes are guided by a curriculum that builds on learners' knowledge and experience and is relevant to the immediate environment. For the minimum standards, the following definitions are used:
  - *learning objectives* identify the knowledge, skills, values and attitudes that will be developed through education activities;
  - *learning content* is the material (knowledge, skills, values and attitudes) to be studied or learned;
  - *teaching methodology* refers to the approach chosen for and used in presenting learning content;
  - *teaching technique or approach* is a component of methodology and constitutes the process used to carry out the overall methodology; and
  - *instructional material* refers to books, posters and other teaching and learning materials.

- **Disaster:** A disaster is a calamitous event resulting in loss of life, great human suffering and distress, and large-scale material damage.[2]

- **Educational activities:** Educational activities are formal and non-formal learning programmes that aim to deliver tangible learning results, with the aim of maintaining continuity in the education of children and youth or providing appropriate learning opportunities for adults.

---

[2] Definition taken from The Sphere Project: *Humanitarian Charter and Minimum Standards in Disaster Response* (2004).

- **Formal education programme:** A formal education programme is a set plan of action to develop a certain level of educational attainment that leads to a recognised certificate. It generally refers to state or national education programmes developed by ministries of education, run through a structured system of state or registered private schools, using a national curriculum or other approved curricula, taught by teachers trained in national teacher training institutions (or private institutions approved by the state), and benefiting from consultation with ministry advisors and inspectors. However, in many emergency situations, formal education, such as for refugee or internally displaced populations, may be set up in a refugee camp and run by implementing partners in conjunction with camp committees, or it may occur in community or religious schools, with the humanitarian community supporting with educational materials and supplies, teacher training and school construction or rehabilitation.

- **Inclusion:** 'Inclusion' refers to the acceptance of all learners in an education programme and the recognition of their equal rights to education.

- **Non-formal education programme:** Non-formal programmes are typically run outside the formal, structured school system and do not necessarily lead to certification or accreditation. However, they may in some cases be attached to schools or included under ministry of education supervision, and learners may use non-formal education programmes as a springboard for late entry into formal education programmes. Such programmes have a plan of action that outlines learning objectives, learning content and instructional materials and are characterised by their variety, flexibility, relevance to specific groups of learners and ability to respond quickly to new educational needs of children or adults. Their curricula range from derivatives of ministry curricula, sometimes delivered in accelerated courses, to entirely new curricula and new approaches to learning.

- **Non-governmental organisations (NGOs):** 'NGOs' refers to organisations, both national and international, which are constituted separately from the government of the country in which they are founded.[3]

- **Other education personnel:** This refers to individuals, other than teachers, who are involved in or assist with an education programme. Such persons may include school supervisors, teacher trainers, education officers, curriculum developers, school clerks and bursars, guards, cooks, and cleaning and maintenance staff, among others.

- **Quality education:** Quality education includes a multitude of elements. These include, but are not limited to: 1) a safe learning environment, 2) competent and well-trained teachers who are knowledgeable in the subject matter, 3) adequate materials for teaching and learning, 4) participatory methods of instruction and 5) reasonable class sizes. Quality education in complex emergencies addresses strategies needed to provide a healing educational environment. There is an emphasis on recreation, play and sport, and the development of related creative activities, as well as the provision of education activities based on reading, writing, numeracy and life skills, so that learners are able to improve not only their cognitive skills, but also prevent a cycle of anger and human destructiveness at a social and generational level.

[3] Ibid.

- **Relevant education:** 'Relevant education' refers to what is learned, how it is learned, and the degree of effective or quality learning. In order to make education relevant, local traditions and institutions, positive cultural practices, belief systems and the needs of the community are integrated into the education programme, including the long-term needs children will have in society in the future, possibly beyond the immediate community.

- **Special education needs:** This term refers to learners with social and cultural disadvantages (including social, religious and economic discrimination) as well as those with specific disabilities (including cognitive, physical or emotional deficits).[4]

- **Stakeholders:** Stakeholders are persons or groups with a common interest in a particular action and its consequences, and who are affected by it.[5]

- **Teacher:** A teacher can be either a formal education programme instructor-educator or a non-formal education programme facilitator or animator, with or without formal training.

[4] Institute for Education Policy Studies: Graduate School of Education and Human Development, *Enhancing Participation, Expanding Access: The Double Axis of Sustainable Educational Development*.
http://www.edpolicy.gwu.edu/resources/enhancing/part_b.html
[5] Welsh, T. and McGinn, N.F. (1998), 'Toward a Methodology of Stakeholder Analysis', in Costin, H. (Ed.) *Readings in Strategy and Strategic Planning*. Dryden Press. Orlando, Florida.

Annex 2: References and Resource Guide

If any of these links do not work, please go to INEE's core reference and advocacy materials page, where links are updated: http://ineesite.org/core/default.asp

General Resources

Aguilar, Pilar and Gonzalo Retamal (1998), *Rapid Educational Response in Complex Emergencies*, Geneva: International Bureau of Education. http://ineesite.org/core/default.asp

Bethke, Lynne and Scott Braunschweig (2004), *Global Survey on Education in Emergencies*, Women's Commission for Refugee Women and Children. http://www.womenscommission.org/pdf/Ed_Emerg.pdf

Boyden, Jo with Paul Ryder (1996), *Implementing the Right to Education in Areas of Armed Conflict*, Oxford. http://meltingpot.fortunecity.com/lebanon/254/boyden.htm

Brookings Institution (1999), *Handbook for Applying the Guiding Principles of Internal Displacement*. http://www.brook.edu/fp/projects/idp/articles/guiding.htm

Crisp, Jeff, Christopher Talbot and Daiana Cipollone (eds.) (2001), *Learning for a Future: Refugee Education in Developing Countries*, Geneva: UNHCR. http://www.unhcr.ch/pubs/epau/learningfuture/learningtoc.htm
• *Education in emergencies* – Margaret Sinclair
• *On school quality and attainment* – James H. Williams
• *Improving quality and attainment in refugee schools: the case of the Bhutanese refugees in Nepal* – Timothy Brown
• *Peace education and refugee youth* – Marc Sommers
• *Vocational training for refugees: a case study from Tanzania* – Erik Lyby

INEE, *Technical Resource Kit for Emergency Education*. http://ineesite.org/about/team_LMR.asp (A digital copy can be ordered free of charge on the INEE website and is included on the INEE CD-ROM Technical Kit.)

Inter-Agency Standing Committee (2002), *Growing the Sheltering Tree: Protecting Rights through Humanitarian Action*. New York: UNICEF. http://www.icva.ch/files/shelteringtree.pdf

Nicolai, Susan (2003), *Education in Emergencies: A Tool Kit for Starting and Managing Education in Emergencies*, Save the Children UK. http://ineesite.org/core/default.asp

Nicolai, Susan and Carl Triplehorn (2003), *The Role of Education in Protecting Children in Conflict*, Humanitarian Practice Network Paper no. 42. http://www.odihpn.org/pdfbin/networkpaper042.pdf

Pigozzi, Mary Jane (1999), *Education in Emergencies and Reconstruction: A Developmental Approach*, Working Paper Series, New York: UNICEF. http://www.unicef.org/girlseducation/EducEmerg.PDF

Sinclair, Margaret (2002), *Planning Education In and After Emergencies, Fundamentals of Educational Planning vol. 73,* Paris: UNESCO IIEP. www.unesco.org/iiep/eng/publications/pubs.htm

Sinclair, Margaret and Carl Triplehorn (2001), *Matrix of Activities and Support Needed for Implementing an Emergency Education Program.* http://www.ineesite.org/core/matrix.asp

Smith, Alan and Tony Vaux (2002), *Education and Conflict,* London: Department for International Development. http://ineesite.org/core/default.asp

Sommers, Marc (2001), *Youth: Care and Protection of Children in Emergencies: A Field Guide,* Save the Children USA. http://ineesite.org/core/default.asp

Sommers, Marc (2002), *Children, Education and War: Reaching Education for All (EFA) Objectives in Countries Affected by Conflict,* World Bank, Conflict Prevention and Reconstruction Unit. http://www.eldis.org/static/DOC15001.htm

Sommers, Marc (2003), *The Education Imperative, Educating Refugee Children,* Academy for Educational Development and Women's Commission for Refugee Women and Children. www.aed.org/ToolsandPublications/upload/EducationImperative.pdf

Sphere Project (2004), *Humanitarian Charter and Minimum Standards in Disaster Response,* Geneva: The Sphere Project. http://www.sphereproject.org

Triplehorn, Carl (2001), *Education: Care and Protection of Children in Emergencies: A Field Guide,* Save the Children USA. http://ineesite.org/core/default.asp

United Nations (1989), Convention on the Rights of the Child, New York, UN. http://www.unhchr.ch/html/menu3/b/k2crc.htm

United Nations (1998), Guiding Principles on Internal Displacement, from UN document E/CN.4/1998/53/Add.2, 11 February 1998. http://www.unhchr.ch/html/menu2/7/b/principles.htm#*

United Nations (2000), Millennium Development Goals, New York, UN. http://www.un.org/millenniumgoals/

United Nations (2000), United Nations Millennium Declaration, New York, UN. http://www.un.org/millennium/declaration/ares552e.htm

UNESCO (2000), *The Dakar Framework for Action: Education for All: Meeting Our Collective Commitments,* derived from the World Education Forum proceedings, Dakar. Paris: UNESCO. http://www.unesco.org/education/efa/ed_for_all/dakfram_eng.shtml

UNESCO (2002), *Education for All: An International Strategy to Put the Dakar Framework for Action on Education for All into Operation,* Paris: UNESCO. http://unesdoc.unesco.org/images/0012/001266/126631eo.pdf

UNESCO (2003), *Guidelines for Education in Situations of Emergency and Crisis: EFA Strategic Planning,* UNESCO. http://unesdoc.unesco.org/images/0012/001282/128214e.pdf

UNESCO (2000), *Thematic Study on Education in Situations of Emergency and Crisis: Assessment EFA 2000,* Paris: UNESCO Emergency Education Assistance Unit. www.unesco.org

UNHCR (1994), *Refugee Children: Guidelines on Protection and Care,* UNHCR. http://www.unhcr.ch

UNHCR (2003), *Revised Education Field Guidelines*, Geneva: UNHCR. http://ineesite.org/core/default.asp

UNHCR (1995), *Revised Guidelines for Educational Assistance to Refugees*, Geneva: UNHCR. http://www.unhcr.ch/

UNHCR and Save the Children (2000), *Action for the Rights of Children (ARC): Education, Critical Issues*, Geneva. http://http://www.unhcr.ch/cgi-bin/texis/vtx/home/opendoc.pdf?tbl=PROTECTION&id=3bb821334&page=PROTECT

UNICEF (1999), *Humanitarian Principles Training: A Child Rights Protection Approach to Complex Emergencies*, UNICEF. http://coe-dmha.org/unicef/unicef2fs.htm

Working Group on Children Affected by Armed Conflict and Displacement (1996), *Promoting Psychosocial Well-Being Among Children Affected by Armed Conflict and Displacement: Principles and Approaches*, Geneva: International Save the Children Alliance. http://www.savethechildren.org/publications/psychsocwellbeing2.pdf

Community Participation

INEE Good Practice Guides – Assessment, Monitoring and Evaluation. http://www.ineesite.org/assess/default.asp

INEE Good Practice Guides – Community Participation in Assessment and Development of Education Programmes. http://www.ineesite.org/assess/com_part.asp

INEE Good Practice Guides – Education Structures and Management: Education Systems Management. http://www.ineesite.org/edstruc/manage.asp

INEE Good Practice Guides – Training and Capacity Building: Community Education Committees. http://www.ineesite.org/training/committee.asp

Jain, S.P and Polman, Wim (2003), *A Handbook for Trainers on Participatory Local Development, FAO Regional Office for Asia and the Pacific*. Bangkok, Thailand. http://www.fao.org/documents/show_cdr.asp?url_file=/DOCREP/006/AD346E/AD346E00.HTM

Shaeffer, Sheldon (1994), *Participation for Educational Change: A Synthesis of Experience*, IIEP, UNESCO. http://www.unesco.org/education/pdf/11_197.pdf

Uemura, Mitsue (1999), *Community Participation in Education: What Do We Know?* HDNED, World Bank. http://poverty.worldbank.org/library/view/14064/

World Health Organisation (1999), *Community Emergency Preparedness: A Manual for Managers and Policy-Makers*, WHO. http://whqlibdoc.who.int/publications/9241545194.pdf

Analysis

Boyden, Jo with Paul Ryder (1996), *Implementing the Right to Education in Areas of Armed Conflict*, Oxford. http://meltingpot.fortunecity.com/lebanon/254/boyden.htm

Gosling, Louisa with Mike Edwards (1995), *Toolkits: A Practical Guide to Assessment, Monitoring, Review and Evaluation*, London, Save the Children.

INEE Good Practice Guides – Assessment, Monitoring and Evaluation.
http://www.ineesite.org/assess/default.asp
• Assessing resource needs and capacities in an initial emergency:
  http://www.ineesite.org/assess/needs.asp
• Assessment of school-age children: http://www.ineesite.org/assess/schoolage.asp
• Assessment of out-of-school youth and youth leaders:
  http://www.ineesite.org/assess/ex_school.asp
• Assessing and analysing community non-formal educational needs:
  http://www.ineesite.org/assess/com_needs.asp
• Partner assessment and selection: http://www.ineesite.org/assess/partner.asp
• Monitoring systems for emergency education: http://www.ineesite.org/assess/monitor.asp
• School data and information systems: http://www.ineesite.org/assess/data.asp

InterAction Working Protection Group (2004), *Making Protection A Priority: A Guidebook for Incorporating Protection into Data Collection in Humanitarian Assistance*, InterAction.
http://www.interaction.org/protection/index.html

Isaac, Annette (2002), *Education, Conflict and Peacebuilding: A Diagnostic Tool*, CIDA.
http://www.acdi-cida.gc.ca/cida_ind.nsf/0/02e83504b7a1b1c085256bb900800f8b?
OpenDocument

Johannessen, Eva Marion (2001), *Guidelines for Evaluation of Education Projects in Emergency Situations*, Oslo, Norwegian Refugee Council.

Nicolai, Susan (2003), 'Steps in Planning' within *Education in Emergencies: A Tool Kit for Starting and Managing Education in Emergencies*, Save the Children UK.
http://www.ineesite.org/core/steps.pdf

Nicolai, Susan and Carl Triplehorn (2003), 'The *immediately, sooner, later* matrix of response'. Annex 1 in *The Role of Education in Protecting Children in Conflict*, Network Paper 42, London: HPN. www.odihpn.org/publist.asp.

OECD (2002), *Glossary of Key Terms in Evaluation and Results-Based Management*, Evaluation and Aid Effectiveness No. 6, Paris: OECD.

Rubin, F. (1995), *A Basic Guide to Evaluation for Development Workers*, Oxford: Oxfam.

Save the Children (2002), *Measuring Change in Education*, SC UK Quality Education Guidelines, London: Save the Children.

Save the Children (2000), *Guidelines for Emergency Preparedness Planning*, London: Save the Children.

Access and Learning Environment

Bergeron, G. and J. Del Rosso (2001), *Food for Education Indicator Guide,* Food and Nutrition Technical Assistance Project, Washington DC, Academy for Educational Development. www.pronutrition.org/files/Food%20for%20Education%20Indicators%20Measurement%20Guide.pdf

Bracken, P. and C. Petty (eds.) (1998), *Rethinking the Trauma of War,* Save the Children.

INEE Good Practice Guides – Assessment, Monitoring and Evaluation
• School site/environmental assessment: http://www.ineesite.org/assess/site.asp

INEE Good Practice Guides – Education Structures and Management
• Clothing and hygiene: http://www.ineesite.org/edstruc/clothing.asp

INEE Good Practice Guides – Inclusive Education
• Toward full participation: http://www.ineesite.org/inclusion/participation.asp
• Gender equality/girls' and women's education: http://www.ineesite.org/inclusion/gender.asp
• Adult ex-combatants and child soldiers: http://www.ineesite.org/inclusion/soldiers.asp
• Children in especially difficult circumstances: http://www.ineesite.org/inclusion/difficult.asp
• Persons with disabilities: http://www.ineesite.org/inclusion/disabled.asp

INEE Good Practice Guides – School Environment and Supplies
• Student learning materials: http://www.ineesite.org/school/materials.asp
• School seating and school furniture: http://www.ineesite.org/school/seating.asp
• School and educational equipment: http://www.ineesite.org/school/equip.asp
• Shelter and school construction: http://www.ineesite.org/school/shelter.asp
• Child-friendly spaces: http://www.ineesite.org/school/friendly.asp
• Safety and security measures: http://www.ineesite.org/school/safety.asp
• Water and sanitation: http://www.ineesite.org/school/water.asp
• School feeding: http://www.ineesite.org/school/feeding.asp

INEE Good Practice Guides – Training and Capacity Building
• The roles of national NGOs: http://www.ineesite.org/training/ngo.asp

Loury, MaryAnne and A. Ager (2001), *The Refugee Experience: Psychosocial Training Module,* Oxford: Refugee Studies Centre, revised edition. http://www.earlybird.qeh.ox.ac.uk/rfgex/

Nicolai, Susan (2003), 'Project Approaches,' within *Education in Emergencies: A Tool Kit for Starting and Managing Education in Emergencies,* Save the Children UK. http://www.ineesite.org/core/approaches.pdf

Tolfree, David (1996), *Restoring Playfulness: Different Approaches to Assisting Children Who Are Psychologically Affected by War or Displacement,* Rädda Barnen, Sweden.

World Food Programme (2001), *School Feeding Works for Girls' Education,* Rome: WFP. www.wfp.org

World Food Programme, *Planning for School Feeding in the Emergency Setting – Situation Analysis, Designing the Programme and Implementation,* WFP. www.wfp.org

World Health Organisation (2003), *Mental Health in Emergencies,* Geneva: WHO. http://www.who.int/disasters/repo/8656.pdf

Teaching and Learning

Baxter, Pamela (2001), INEE Peace Education Kit, within the *Technical Resource Kit for Emergency Education,* INEE. http://www.ineesite.org/about/team_LMR.asp (A digital copy can be ordered free of charge on the INEE website and is included on the INEE CD-ROM Technical Kit.)

Boyden, Jo with Paul Ryder (1996), *Implementing the Right to Education in Areas of Armed Conflict,* Oxford. http://meltingpot.fortunecity.com/lebanon/254/boyden.htm

Brochmann, Helge et al (2001), *Human Rights: A Teacher's Guide,* Oslo: Norwegian Refugee Council. http://ineesite.org/core/default.asp

Bush, Kenneth D. and Diana Saltarelli (eds.) (2000), *The Two Faces of Education in Ethnic Conflict: Towards a Peacebuilding Education For Children,* UNICEF Innocenti Insight. http://www.unicef-icdc.org/publications/pdf/insight4.pdf

INEE Good Practice Guides – Educational Content and Methodology
· Training teachers to meet psychosocial needs: http://www.ineesite.org/edcon/psy_soc.asp
· Curriculum and testing: http://www.ineesite.org/edcon/curriculum.asp
· Revising and negotiating the curriculum: http://www.ineesite.org/edcon/revise_curr.asp
· Life skills and complementary education programmes (health education, landmine awareness, peace education): http://www.ineesite.org/edcon/life_skills.asp
· Early childhood development: http://www.ineesite.org/edcon/early.asp
· Secondary school education: http://www.ineesite.org/edcon/second.asp
· Tertiary education – university, colleges and vocational schools: http://www.ineesite.org/edcon/tertiary.asp
· Community information campaigns: http://www.ineesite.org/edcon/com_info.asp
· Adult education: http://www.ineesite.org/edcon/adult.asp
· Out-of-school programmes: http://www.ineesite.org/edcon/out_school.asp

INEE Good Practice Guides – Education Structures and Management
· School administration: http://www.ineesite.org/edstruc/admin.asp

INEE Good Practice Guides – School Environment and Supplies
· School supplies and teaching materials: http://www.ineesite.org/school/supplies.asp

INEE Learning Materials Task Group (2001), *Teaching – Learning Materials for Education in Situations of Emergency and Crisis: An Overview,* INEE. www.ineesite.org

Inter-Agency Standing Committee (2003), *Revised Guidelines for HIV/AIDS Interventions in Emergency Settings,* United Nations. http://www.humanitarianinfo.org/iasc/IASC%20products/FinalGuidelines17Nov2003.pdf

Lorey, Mark (2001), *Child Soldiers: Care and Protection for Children in Emergencies: A Field Guide,* Save the Children USA. http://ineesite.org/core/default.asp

Lowicki, Jane (2000), *Untapped Potential: Adolescents Affected by Armed Conflict. A Review of Programs and Policies,* Women's Commission for Refugee Women and Children.

Lowicki, Jane (2004), *Youth Speak Out: New Voices on the Protection and Participation of Young People Affected by Armed Conflict,* Women's Commission for Refugee Women and Children. http://www.womenscommission.org/pdf/cap_youth.pdf

Lowicki, Jane (2004), *Reference Guide: Adolescent and Youth Education,* Women's Commission for Refugee Women and Children. http://www.womenscommission.org/pdf/cap_ones.pdf

McConnan, Isobel and S. Uppard (2001), *Children Not Soldiers: Guidelines for Working with Child Soldiers and Children Associated with Fighting Forces,* London: Save the Children. http://www.reliefweb.int/library/documents/2002/sc-children-dec01.htm

Nicolai, Susan (2003), 'Framework for Learning' within *Education in Emergencies: A Tool Kit for Starting and Managing Education in Emergencies,* Save the Children UK. http://www.ineesite.org/core/framework.pdf

Norwegian Refugee Council (with UNESCO-PEER) (2000), *Teacher Emergency Package: Teacher's Guide: Basic Literacy, Numeracy and Themes for Everyday Living,* Norwegian Refugee Council, Oslo. http://ineesite.org/about/TTLMBKLT.pdf

Norwegian Refugee Council (2000), *Teacher Emergency Package: Trainer's Support Manual,* Norwegian Refugee Council. http://ineesite.org/about/TTLMBKLT.pdf

Norwegian Refugee Council (2001), *Strategies: Spearheading Core Activities in Phases of Conflict.* One organisation's definition of emergency scenarios and programming opportunities. http://www.ineesite.org/core/core_act1.asp

Save the Children (1999), *Mines – Beware! Starting to Teach Children Safe Behaviour,* Rädda Barnen, Sweden.

Tawil, Sobhi and Alexandra Harley (2002), *Curriculum Change and Social Cohesion in Conflict-Affected Societies,* report of technical meeting, UNESCO IBE. http://www.see-educoop.net/education_in/pdf/curric_change_social_cohesion-bih_enl_t05.pdf

Tawil, Sobhi and Alexandra Harley (eds.) (2004), *Education, Conflict and Social Cohesion (Studies in Comparative Education),* Geneva: UNESCO IBE.

UNESCO, *Teacher Emergency Package (TEP)* with links to the TEP for Angola and the UNICEF-UNESCO TEP Programme in Rwanda. http://portal.unesco.org/education/en/ev.php-URL_ID=13446&URL_DO=DO_TOPIC&URL_SECTION=201.html

UNHCR (2001), *HIV/AIDS Education for Refugee Youth: The Window of Hope,* Geneva: UNHCR.

UNICEF, *International Guidelines for Landmine and Unexploded Ordnance Awareness Education,* New York, UNICEF. http://members.iinet.net.au/~pictim/mines/unicef/mineawar.pdf

UNICEF, UNESCO, WHO and the World Bank (2000), *Focusing Resources on Effective School Health: A FRESH Start to Enhancing the Quality and Equity of Education,* New York: UNICEF. http://unesdoc.unesco.org/images/0012/001240/124086mo.pdf

Welbourn, Alice (1995), *Stepping Stones: A Training Package on HIV/AIDS, Communication and Relationship Skills,* London: ActionAid. http://www.steppingstonesfeedback.org/index.htm

Teachers and Other Education Personnel

INEE Good Practice Guides – Assessment, Monitoring and Evaluation
• Assessment of teacher/facilitator availability and capacity, including selection:
  http://www.ineesite.org/assess/teacher.asp

INEE Good Practice Guides – Education Structures and Management
• School administration: http://www.ineesite.org/edstruc/admin.asp
• Compensation and payment of education staff: http://www.ineesite.org/edstruc/payment.asp

INEE Good Practice Guides – Training and Capacity Building
• Certification and accreditation: http://www.ineesite.org/training/certificate.asp

Inter-Agency Standing Committee (2002), *Plan of Action and Core Principles of Codes of Conducts on Protection from Sexual Abuse and Exploitation in Humanitarian Crisis*, United Nations. http://www.humanitarianinfo.org/iasc/poasexualexploitation.doc

Policy and Coordination

INEE Good Practice Guides – Education Structures and Management
• School fees: http://www.ineesite.org/edstruc/fees.asp
• Repatriation and reintegration: http://www.ineesite.org/edstruc/repatriate.asp

INEE Good Practice Guides – Training and Capacity Building
• Pre-service, in-service, in the school: http://www.ineesite.org/training/service.asp
• Teacher observation and lesson planning: http://www.ineesite.org/training/observation.asp
• On-site teacher training and support – mobile trainers and mentors:
  http://www.ineesite.org/training/on_site.asp
• The role of national government: http://www.ineesite.org/training/government.asp
• The roles of international NGOs: http://www.ineesite.org/training/int_ngo.asp
• The roles of UN agencies: http://www.ineesite.org/training/un.asp

Sommers, Marc (2004), *Co-ordinating Education During Emergencies and Reconstruction: Challenges and Responsibilities*, Education in Emergencies and Reconstruction: Thematic Policy Studies. Paris: UNESCO IIEP.

Annex 3: Acknowledgements

INEE Working Group on Minimum Standards for Education in Emergencies
CARE Canada (Nancy Drost) * CARE USA (Hassan Mohammed) * Catholic Relief Services
(Mike Pozniak and Christine Carneal) * International Rescue Committee (Rebecca Winthrop and
Wendy Smith) * Norwegian Church Aid (Birgit Villumstad) * Norway UN Association/
Norwegian Refugee Council (Helge Brochmann) * Refugee Education Trust (Tim Brown) * Save
the Children UK (Susan Nicolai) * Save the Children USA (Christine Knudsen) * UNESCO
(Christopher Talbot) * UNHCR (Nemia Temporal) * UNICEF (Pilar Aguilar) * World
Education/The Consortium (Fred Ligon)

Transition team for establishing a Working Group on Minimum Standards
CARE USA (Jane Benbow) * Catholic Relief Services (Mike Pozniak) * Inter-Agency Network for
Education in Emergencies (Nancy Drost) * The International Rescue Committee (Wendy Smith)
* Norwegian Refugee Council (Eldrid Midttun) * Save the Children Alliance (Susan Nicolai) *
Save the Children USA (Christine Knudsen)

Donors to the minimum standards process
Canadian International Development Agency (CIDA) * International Rescue Committee *
International Save the Children Alliance * Save the Children Norway * Swedish International
Development Cooperation Agency (SIDA) * UNESCO * UNHCR * UNICEF * USAID * World Bank

INEE Steering Group members
CARE International * International Rescue Committee * International Save the Children
Alliance * Norwegian Refugee Council * UNESCO * UNHCR * UNICEF * World Bank

INEE Secretariat
Allison Anderson, Focal Point on Minimum Standards (hosted by the International Rescue
Committee)
Beverly Roberts, Network Coordinator (hosted by UNESCO)
Goeril Tomren, Assistant Network Coordinator (hosted by UNESCO)

INEE Donors
CARE USA * The International Save the Children Alliance * The Mellon Foundation * Norwegian
Agency for Development (NORAD) * Norwegian Ministry of Foreign Affairs * UNESCO *
UNHCR * UNICEF * World Bank

Regional Consultation Delegates
*=Consultation Host
(OC)=Regional Consultation Organising Committee member

*Africa Collective Consultation (Nairobi, Kenya, 21-23 January 2004, hosted by CARE Canada
and Norwegian Church Aid)*: Catherine Arnesen, Norwegian Refugee Council, Liberia; Jean-Marie
Mukoka Betukameso, Service Centrale Education à la Vie/UNFPA, DRC; Mudiappasamy
Devadoss, Ph.D., UNESCO PEER, Kenya; Mike Foley, Jesuit Refugee Services, Sudan; Martha
Hewison, Windle Trust International/Hugh Pilkington Charitable Trust, Uganda; Vick Shiverenje

Ikobwa, UNHCR Kenya; Joyce Ishengoma, CARE Tanzania; Davidson Oboyah Jonah, Christian Children's Fund Sierra Leone; Celestin Kamori Banga, Norwegian Refugee Council DRC; M.R. Warue Kariuki (OC), Save the Children UK, Kenya; Thomas Ngolo Katta, Center for the Coordination of Youth Activities, Sierra Leone; Levi Khamis, Norwegian Church Aid; Yoboue N'da Kouassi, Ministry of Education, Cote d'Ivoire; Nderikyo Elizabeth Ligate, Southern Africa Extension Unit, Tanzania; Elena Locatelli, AVSI (Associazione Volontari Servizio Internazionale) Northern Uganda; Gilbert Sanya Lukhoba, Windle Trust Kenya; Changu Mannathoko (OC), UNICEF, Southern and Eastern Africa (Africa Organising Committee member); Walter Matoke, Consultant; Clement Mhlanga, Save the Children UK, Zimbabwe; Carlinda Maria Rodrigues Monteiro, Christian Children's Fund Angola; Neema Ndayishimiye, Ministry for National Education, Burundi; Marangu Njogu, CARE Kenya; Mima Perisic, UNICEF Sudan; Jolly Rubagiza, Kigali Institute of Education; Ibrahim Mohamed Said, Ministry of Education, Somaliland; Seny Sylla, Ministry of Education, Guinea; Christiana Thorpe, Forum for African Women Educationalists, Sierra Leone; David Walker (OC), International Rescue Committee Sierra Leone; Joyce Wanican, International Rescue Committee Uganda; John Yuggu Tileyi, Catholic Relief Services Sudan; Kassaye Yimer, CARE Ethiopia
INEE Working Group and Steering Group representatives: Allison Anderson, INEE; Pamela Baxter, UNHCR; Helge Brochmann, Norwegian Refugee Council; Tim Brown, Refugee Education Trust; Christine Carneal, Catholic Relief Services; Nancy Drost*, CARE Canada; Beverly Roberts, INEE; Birgit H. Villumstad*, Norwegian Church Aid

Asia and Pacific Collective Consultation *(Kathmandu, Nepal, 21-23 April 2004, hosted by the International Save the Children Alliance)*: Emmanuelle Abrioux (OC)*, Save the Children, Nepal; Feny de los Angeles-Bautista, Community of Learners Foundation and Philippine Children's Television Foundation; Steve Aswin, UNICEF Indonesia; Ranjinie Chandrika Jayewardene, Commonwealth Education Fund, Sri Lanka; Helina Alia Dost, International Rescue Committee Pakistan; Uaiporn Daodueanchai, Consortium Thailand (World Education and World Learning); Seema Gaikwad, Sphere India; Abdul Ghaffar, Save the Children USA, Pakistan; Dr. Abdul Samad Ghafoori, UNICEF Afghanistan; Roza Gul, Ockenden International, Pakistan; Mir Abdul Malik Hashemi, GTZ BEFARe (Basic Education For Afghan Refugees), Pakistan; Ung Ngo Hok, Ministry of Education, Youth and Sport, Cambodia; A.Z.M. Sakhawat Hossain, BRAC Education Program, Government of Bangladesh Partnership Unit; Teresita G. Inciong, Department of Education, Government of the Philippines; Shakir Ishaq, BEFARe, Pakistan; Ingrid Iversen, International Institute for Educational Planning (IIEP) UNESCO; Umesh Kumar Kattel, World Health Organisation, Nepal; Laxman Khanal, Department of Education, Government of Nepal; Chirharu Kondu, UNICEF Nepal; Samphre Llalungpa, UNICEF Nepal; Udaya Manandhar, Save the Children USA, Nepal; Rachel McKinney (OC), International Rescue Committee Afghanistan; N. Vinod Chandra Menon (OC), UNICEF India; Geeta S. Menon, CARE India; Abdul Azis Muslim, Non Violence International and Aceh Peace Education Program; Janardhan Nepal, Department of Education, Government of Nepal; Patricia Omidian, Quaker Service, Afghanistan; W. Sterling Perera, Education Consultant, Sri Lanka; Anna Pinto, CORE (Centre for Organisation Research and Education), India; Loknath Pokhrel, CARITAS Nepal; N.M. Prusty, Sphere India and CARE India; Alexandra Pura, Oxfam Great Britain, Philippines Office; Kasturi Sengupta, Catholic Relief Services, India; Helen Sherpa, World Education, Nepal; Anil Sharma, Department of Education, Government of Nepal; Sanjay Singh, Catholic Relief Services, India; Deepesh Sinha, Disaster Mitigation Institute, Gujarat, India; Sarah Smith, Concern Bangladesh; Marc van der Stouwe,

ZOA Refugee Care, Thailand; Dr. Sudiono, Ministry of Education, Indonesia; Anne Thomas, Education and Community Development Consultant, Cambodia; Leela Raj Upadhyay, World Food Program, Nepal
INEE Working Group representatives: Allison Anderson, INEE; Helge Brochmann, Norwegian Refugee Council; Christine Knudsen, Save the Children US*; Fred Ligon, Consortium Thailand (World Education and World Learning); Susan Nicolai*, Save the Children UK; Michael Pozniak, Catholic Relief Services; Carl Triplehorn, Save the Children US*

Latin America and Caribbean Collective Consultation (Panama City, Panama 5-7 May 2004, hosted by UNICEF): Fernando Jiovani Arias Morales, Fundación Dos Mundos, Colombia; Luis Yezid Beltran Bautista, Project Counseling Service, Colombia; Carmen Liliana Bieberach, Fundación para la Igualdad de Oportunidades, Panama; Roy Bowen, UNICEF Belize; Juan Pablo Bustamante, UNICEF Ecuador; Claudia Beatriz Cárdenas Becerra, SPM Latinoamérica Consultores S.A Estrategia Internacional; Claudia Ernestina Carrillo Ramírez, Comité de Familiares de Víctimas del "Caracazo" febrero de 1989, Venezuela; Milton Xavier Castellanos Mosquera, ICRC, Panama; Joseph Marc Cesar, Ministry of Education and Culture, Haiti; Renee Cuijpers, UNHCR Panama; Iris Isalia Currillo de Reyes, Ministry of Education, El Salvador; Victoria Ginja, World Food Programme, Panama; Diego Vidal Gutiérrez Santos, Ministry of Education, Government of Panama; Nirvah Jean-Jacques (OC), The Haitian Foundation for Private Education (FONHEP), Haiti; Francis Joseph, Christian Children's Fund, Dominica and St Vincent; Gustave Joseph, Ministry of Education and Culture, Haiti; Reyes Jiménez, SINAPROC, Panama; Martha Llanos, PhD; Education and Human Development Specialist; Garren Lumpkin (OC)*, UNICEF TACRO, Panama; Gladys Maria Minaya Urena, Ministry of Education, Dominican Republic; Marina Rocío Mojica Carvajal, Save the Children UK, Colombia; Maria Paz Bermeja, UNHCR SURGE, Panama; Richard Pelczar, UNESCO; Gerardo Perez Holguin (OC), CEDEDIS-Corporation for Community Development and Social Integration, Colombia; Nidya Quiroz (OC)*, UNICEF-TACRO Consuelo Ramirez, Secretaria de Educacion Publica, Mexico; Flor Alba Romero Medina, Universidad Nacional de Colombia; Raisa Ruiz, UNICEF Panama; Unai Sacona Benegas, UNICEF Dominican Republic; Anyoli Sanabria Lopez, UNICEF Nicaragua; José Alejandro Santander Narvaez, Organización Panamericana de la Salud, Ecuador; Yasuhiro Taniguchi, UN OCHA, Panama; David Martin Villarroel García (OC), Save The Children Alliance, Bolivia; Miloody Phaine Vincent, Ministry of Education and Culture, Haiti; Sofia Westberg, UNICEF Peru
INEE Working Group representatives: Allison Anderson, INEE; Marina Lopez Anselme, Refugee Education Trust; Rebecca Winthrop, IRC

Middle East, North Africa and Europe Collective Consultation (Amman, Jordan, 19-21 May 2004, co-hosted by UNESCO and UNHCR): Nader Anton Abu Amsha, East Jerusalem YMCA Rehabilitation Program and YMCA Beit-Sahour; Ziad Abu Laban, International Committee of the Red Cross (ICRC), Jerusalem; Pushpa Acharya, World Food Programme, Middle East, Central Asia and Eastern Europe, Egypt; Inna Kimaevna Airapetyan, CARE North Caucasus, Chechnya; Fayez Ahmad Al-Fasfous, Early Childhood Resource Centre, West Bank; Steven Anderson, ICRC, Jerusalem; Staneala M. Beckley (OC), UNICEF Middle East and North Africa Region, Jordan; Khoudja Beldjilali, Ministry of Education, Algeria; Leila Boumghar, Ministry of Education, Algeria; Yaser Mohamed Daoud, Nabaa Lebanon; Veronique Ehlen, UNHCR Jordan; Malika Elatifi, Save the Children, Morocco; Holly Hughson, University of California at Berkeley; Shaikh Kabiroddin, UN Relief and Works Agency for Palestine Refugees in the Far East (UNRWA); Doris Knoechel

(OC), World Vision International; Zahra Mirghani (OC)*, UNHCR, Lebanon; Dr. Ahmed Mirza Mirza, Saladhaddin University, Iraq; Robert Mizzi (OC), Kosovo Educator Development Project; Issa Nassar, Ministry of Education, Government of Jordan; Robert Parua (OC)*, UNESCO Jordan; Jacqueline Peters, UNICEF Jordan; Amela Piric, Organisation for Security & Cooperation in Europe, Sarajevo; Shao Potung, UNICEF Occupied Palestinian Territory; Basri A.S. Salmoodi, Ministry of Education and Higher Education, Palestinian Authority; Kabir Shaikh, UNRWA, Jordan; Adina Shapiro, Middle East Children's Association, Israel; Aferdita Spahiu, UNICEF Kosovo; Martine Storti, Ministry of Education, France; Mohammed Tarakhan, UNRWA, Jordan; Geeta Verma, UNICEF Jordan; Jamie Williams (OC), Save the Children UK, Egypt; Isuf Zeneli, Ministry of Education, Science and Technology, Kosovo

INEE Working Group on Minimum Standards and Steering Group representatives: Allison Anderson, INEE; Eldrid Midttun, NRC; Susan Nicolai, Save the Children UK; Beverly Roberts, INEE; Christopher Talbot*, UNESCO IIEP; Nemia Temporal*, UNHCR

Peer Review Facilitator: Joan Sullivan-Owomoyela
Peer Review Analysis Consultant: Margaret Sinclair
Minimum Standards Intern: Christine Pagen
INEE gratefully acknowledges the assistance of the Academy for Educational Development and the Global Learning Portal in the peer review process.

Peer Reviewers: Chris Berry, UK Department for International Development (DFID); Lynne Bethke, InterWorks; Marilyn Blaeser, CARE; Beverlee Bruce, Social Science Research Council; Peter Buckland, World Bank; Dana Burde, Columbia University; Jim DiFrancesca, Harvard University; Eric Eversman, Consultant; Jan Field, UNHCR; Sarah Dryden Peterson, Harvard University/Makerere University; Jason Hart, Oxford; Martha Hewison, Windle Trust; Dorothy Jobolingo, International Rescue Committee Uganda; Alison Joyner, Sphere; Ellen Van Kalmthout, UNICEF; Jackie Kirk, McGill University; Jane Lowicki, International Rescue Committee; Gilberto Mendez, Christian Children's Fund (CCF); Eldrid Midttun, NRC; Micheal Montgomery, CIDA; Claus Nelson, Red Barnet; John Rhodes Paige, St. Edwards; Delia Rarela-Barcelona, UNFPA; Margaret Sinclair, Consultant; Marc Sommers, Consultant; Martine Storti, Ministry of Education, France; Carl Triplehorn, Save the Children US; Julian Watson, Consultant; Michael Wessells, CCF and Randolf Macon; Jim Williams, George Washington University; Sharon Wright, CARE Sudan Basic Education Program/University of Massachusetts; and all WGMSEE members.

INEE's WGMSEE is also grateful for the guidance of the Sphere Project staff, with special thanks to Nan Buzard and Alison Joyner.

Handbook Editor: David Wilson

While INEE gratefully acknowledges the contribution of everyone who participated in the local consultation process, INEE list-serve consultations and feedback on the MSEE, it would take more than 20 pages to list individual names, and space does not allow this. However, a full listing of all contributors can be found on the INEE website at: http://www.ineesite.org/standards/msee.asp, as well as on the MSEE CD-ROM, which is available through the website.

INEE Minimum Standards for Education in Emergencies
Feedback form

All comments submitted will be kept on file with the INEE Focal Point on Minimum Standards and will be reviewed for future web-based revisions and in case of a further revised hard copy edition in the future.

Name:

Job title and organisation:

Address:

Phone/e-mail:

Date:

In responding to the following questions, please be specific, and where possible, provide evidence-based background or references for your suggestion.

1) What general comments or feedback do you have on any part of the INEE Handbook on Minimum Standards for Education in Emergencies?

2) Are there indicators that need adjusting?

3) Is there new information that should be reflected in the guidance notes?

4) Are there additional tools that should be listed as appendices or within the References and Resource Guide Annex?

Please send this form to the INEE Focal Point on Minimum Standards for Education in Emergencies: Allison Anderson
c/o International Rescue Committee / 122 East 42nd Street / New York, NY 10168-1289
Tel: (+1 212) 551 3107 / Fax: (+1 212) 551 3185 / allison@theirc.org

For more information on INEE and/or the minimum standards process, please visit the website at http://www.ineesite.org